A Chance At Life

Stories of Inspiration and Hope for Foster and Adoptive Parents of Abused Children

Elaine Rose Penn

© Copyright 2010, Elaine Rose Penn

All Rights Reserved.

No part of this book may be reproduced, stored in a
retrieval system, or transmitted by any means,
electronic, mechanical, photocopying, recording,
or otherwise, without written permission
from the author.

ISBN: 978-0-9700449-1-4

This book is lovingly dedicated to

Cetra ("Cee")

Not flesh of my flesh, nor bone of my bone, but still miraculously my own. Never forget – not for a minute – you weren't born under my heart but in it.
The Adoption Creed

Table of Contents

Preface		vii
Acknowledgements		ix
Chapter 1	Fighting to Live	1
Chapter 2	Secrets	3
Chapter 3	Losing Both Parents	6
Chapter 4	Safe Risks	10
Chapter 5	Dolls, Dolls, Everywhere	18
Chapter 6	They Are Never Truly Yours	21
Chapter 7	Eating in the Basement With Dogs	27
Chapter 8	Tupac	31
Chapter 9	Teasing: The Peculiar Domain of Children	34
Chapter 10	A Parent's Dream	37
Chapter 11	Cetra, the Little Dictator	40
Chapter 12	Forgiveness	44
Chapter 13	A Light At Dusk	49
Chapter 14	Poogie Bear and a Doll Named Annie	53
Chapter 15	One Fine Day	60
Chapter 16	Letting Go is a Process	66
Chapter 17	A Good, Hard Cry	71
Chapter 18	A Community of Healers	78

Preface

Writing and compiling *A Chance At Life* took a surprisingly emotional toll. Some stories reduced me to tears as I wrote them; while others made me laugh. Still, I feel an exhilarating accomplishment at having shared some of my most private memories about the life I shared with Cetra.

I have deliberately left out certain details about her warden state and some details about her natural parents in an attempt to protect Cetra's privacy as well as that of her birthparents. New York State, which is the state she and I resided in, was never her warden state.

While I have shared some of the details of Cetra's early childhood abuse, the worst of it, I have deliberately left out. When she came to me, I was told that at the time she was placed in my custody, she was one of the worse cases of child abuse in that state. I am sure that since that time, they have seen still worse than Cetra. I was informed that some of her foster parents as well as other foster children had actively and maliciously participated in both her mental and physical abuse.

You will find most of the stories poignant, perhaps difficult to read without tears. I have not shared them to evoke sympathy, as much as to prove how possible it is to turn horrific pain into conquest. Every life has stories. Cetra's life stories could have ended with grave failure and even death. As destiny would have it, the stories of abuse are only a small portion of the full testament that will yet describe her life. With God's help, and the assistance of a community of helpers and friends, her past life now includes whole chapters of stories marked by strong and affirming love as well as triumph.

I was not by any means the model adoptive parent, as you will surmise in reading this collection. I did and do, however, love this child with my whole heart and being. I hope that what I learned along the way and the sharing of these stories will in some way help you whether you are currently an adoptive parent, thinking of becoming one, or looking for another level of insight in trying to become a better parent to your own natural child. ♪♫♪

Elaine Rose Penn, Author

Acknowledgements

There are three specific people to whom I owe a debt of gratitude with respect to this book: Timothy and Rochelle Fowler; and Elaine Patrice Perkins. Thank you so much for your words of counsel and encouragement – and for believing in me…

Finally… to the employees of the New York State Comptroller's Office, thank you for insisting that I do this.

Elaine Rose

Chapter 1 - Fighting to Live

Life is filled with so many contrasts, perplexities and ironies that in my reflective moments, I am often filled with awe and even reverence. The things that would appear to have no rhyme, end up revealing great reason; and the things that twist and spiral out of control, can suddenly turn in one specific direction and become steady on a clear path. People who don't believe in destiny or life purpose must spend most of their lives in the same cave. There is no way you can look at the mysterious nuances of life and not appreciate the undercurrent of Divine direction.

Allegedly, Cetra's abuse began shortly after her birth, but she wasn't supposed to live in the first place. She was born a premie, having been born two or three months ahead of time. I am told that she was born weighing one pound, and you could have held her entire being in the palm of your hand.

The most vivid report I have of her determination to face this world in spite of her baby-sorrows and struggle for survival came from Cetra's doctors. During the first year of her life, she had numerous breathing difficulties, ear infections, and suffered from one bout of pneumonia after another. I can remember getting these reports of her natal struggle and just breaking down in tears. I had never even seen her at the point of her birth, or picked her up, or had the opportunity to kiss her little face. It sounds odd, I know, but even then, it felt like she belonged to me. Would you believe that during the entire time she was in my care, except for a few minor colds, she was never sick a day in her life? Perhaps God decided that she had suffered enough.

After living her first year of life dependent on machines, cords, and injections, I remember one memorable occasion when my mother called to give me the newest report of her life-struggle. Every call was a nightmare. I never knew if the report was going to be that she had finally died, or what. They had already tried to prepare my mother for the worse. I can vividly recall the report on this particular occasion that would change my sorrow forever and provide for me a lifeline of hope regarding Cetra's fate.

She had been moved out of one medical facility and placed in a Catholic Hospital. The nuns there provided her round-the-clock, intensive monitoring and care. Although I was initially concerned that they had moved her at all, I heard the words of hope from them that I needed to hear in order to cope with her life's struggle.

The doctors reported to my mother that although they didn't understand it, my tiny little misshapen Cetra was fighting to live. In spite of her bruising, her rude and too-early introduction to the world, and the odds that seemed stacked against her...she was fighting to live anyway.

That something that was bred into Cetra before she was even conceived was something that I watched grow and flourish in her during the years she was in my care and custody. She never stopped fighting to live...to find a place in a normal world that had early-on determined her to be abnormal. ♪

Inspiration and Hope

The fact that your adoptive child has survived everything they've gone through, points to the strength of the destiny that lies within that child.

Look for the areas of your child's creativity and water them lavishly. What was meant for destruction may very well turn out for the greatest good.

Chapter 2 - Secrets

Before Cetra was born, she had a brother who died in a mysterious manner. There was an investigation done, but the full truth of what happened to him was never disclosed. The only thing we really ever knew of his life and death was that he died before he was even given a chance to make a contribution to the world.

Cetra would often bring up his name to me and I participated as an unwilling conspirator in the secrets surrounding his sudden death. Funny little Cetra always referred to him as her "baby" brother. I could never get through to her that he would have been her big brother and not the other way around. In her mind, he was forever fixed at the stage of life when he died – as a baby.

Once or twice, Cetra's birth parents had taken her to the place of his burial. As her custodial parent, I always resented the fact that my child had to be introduced to death in this rather unfeeling place of grass, granite stone, and inscriptions. In her mind, this place would be the only picture and representation she would have of her mysterious brother.

I always successfully skirted the issue of his birth and death because I really did not have many facts about either. I once saw a bad picture of him; but oddly enough, no one had ever taken baby pictures of him for display. I even found his name odd, but who was I to judge? Cetra would have neither a picture of his face nor an explanation about his name – just an indelible memory of him as a place and a thing with his odd name inscribed thereon.

Whenever she would mention him, she would blurt it out quite unexpectedly and I could never identify any specific thing that seemed to bring him to her mind. The secret of his death became, really, a secret about his existence. Had he really ever even lived? Why had he even been born into the world to die so quickly and without explanation? I was as mystified as Cetra. Whenever Cetra brought up his name, I felt his gravestone gnawing at my conscience. Just the secret itself seemed to feed her curiosity.

Secrets. Wouldn't it be nice if only the people who share them or know of them could be hurt by the real facts? There is another possible set of victims. They are the people excluded from knowing the facts of the secrets, but who find out anyway and who resent the deception because they weren't told the facts when they were young enough to forgive. ♪

Inspiration and Hope

As an adoptive parent, there will be very few secrets you will come to know about regarding your child. To one extent, this is good, but to another extent, this is tough.

Be grateful that there are some things that you will never know.

If, by occasion and circumstances, you learn some secrets, be very careful how you share them, especially with your child. If sharing them will bring your child peace, and you know that your child will eventually find out anyway, choose your time and place well. Some things children can accept a whole lot better in their youth than they will once they become older.

When sharing or explaining information to them, speak what you know with word pictures, and don't be afraid to edit out information that will hurt them rather than help. This includes information that they are too young to place in a proper mental and life experience perspective. In other words, there is some information that we, as adults, process in terms of our life's experiences and our maturity. Children don't have this. So, if you share information that they have not developed the capacity to receive and process, you will create dark shadows in their thinking.

Some things can be told now, while other things can wait until they are older. You must think through and identify information that should never be shared at all. Lastly, as you think through what you will share and what you will edit, remember that there is a difference between a fact and "the truth." What is revealed to you as the adoptive parent in the form of "facts," may not necessarily constitute the "truth" of what happened.

In exposing secrets to your child, speak to them with gentle frankness and directness, but don't forget that you are an adult talking to a child. Decide ahead of time what you will share and what you will withhold, and don't let your child convince you that they are old enough to handle more.

Chapter 3 - Losing Both Parents

I am very blessed that both of my parents are still alive. For years, I even enjoyed the generational fellowship of my great grandmother and my grandfather. Longevity is a gift on both sides of my parent's families. Hence, I can't entirely understand the feeling of losing both parents for a young child. What I have come to understand in raising Cetra, is that death is not the only way to lose a parent. They can simply not be around for the sacred moments of life, and that is as much death as the coldness of the grave.

When Cetra came to me, the warden state that she lived in had been negligent in terminating one parent's rights. This caused huge problems for me in obtaining guardianship. As I tried to pursue action against her birthparents in the New York State system, I kept hitting one wall after another. I needed the warden state that had taken custody of her to do this dirty work. In the end, it meant having to play a waiting game that Cetra did not comprehend. Can you imagine having to do critical things like enrolling your child in school, obtaining vital records of her birth and medical history with a letter written on business stationary? Literally all I had for many years was this letter written by her caseworker in the warden state. Few people asked to see it, and in my reflective moments, it disturbs me a little that nobody cared to make sure that this child was in my custody legally.

When she came to me, she hated one of her parents. I remember arguing with the New York State caseworker who felt that she had a right to hate. I almost threw the woman out of my house. In my home, Cetra would never be allowed to hate. I didn't have to read a book to know that when a child grows up hating their parents, they will always have dysfunctional relationships with every human being in their life. My first order of business, I knew, would be to root out this stem of hatred and teach her the power and language of forgiveness. I knew I needed to do it during these pre-adolescent years, because once she became an adult, it would be next to impossible to chisel through the hardened animosity and bitterness.

To do that, I took upon myself the hatred, anger, and disappointment that Cetra felt towards both of her parents. I did what I read in the Holy Scriptures that Christ had done for us. At first, the little girl in her who had been taught immediate submission to adults balked at the idea. I kept prodding her to reassure her that I wanted her to tell me everything and say whatever she wanted – I wanted her to express the contents of her heart. I wanted her to spew out all of the poison in its fullness onto me. The only way that we could face the devastating loss of both parents together – was to face the agonizing ugliness of what had happened to her – together. Yes, you got it right…I told her to speak to me as if I were the parent she was so angry with.

Guess what I found? I found that I was big enough to handle her little girl pain. I found that there was nothing that she could say to me that I could not bear to hear. I found that hearing her pain did not beat me down nor make me feel victimized by it. In fact, once I got her to a place that she freely talked about her experiences, it empowered me as the parent who stayed.

I taught her, through acceptance, love, laughter and hope, that not all parents abandon their children. I taught her that she could go to sleep at night without the fear that someone would come and take her away or move her to a new and strange household without her say. I taught her that she was safe with me.

On the day that I got the official paper that I had been waiting for five years to receive, I felt a mixture of emotions and they all hit me at once. I laughed and cried at the same time. In bold black letters, the official document from her warden state announced that I now had full guardianship rights over my child. Cetra, being Cetra, gave me a completely different reaction. When I sat with her on this momentous occasion to share the good news, she looked at me quizzically and asked me what all of it meant. When I tried to explain, she still didn't get it and after a few moments, shook her head at me the way teenagers do when they think their parents are weird. Then, she left me there in tears and in a state of gratitude that I felt but could not express.

My funny Cetra...she didn't have a clue about what the paper meant, because I had never allowed her to feel like a ward – or an orphan. I never wanted her to feel that I was in any way not her mother, or that someone including a faceless governmental bureaucracy could simply decide to come and take her away.

When she left my life, one of the hardest things I ever had to do with respect to her, besides allowing her to go, was to take her off of my insurance plan as my dependent. She had always been mine, and I had always been hers. Mostly, I don't know what has become of her or even if she is being taken care of. What I do know for sure is that you don't have to bear a child to be that child's parent – I will always be Cetra's parent. Blood may be thicker than water, but some things are thicker than blood. ♪

Inspiration & Hope

If you are going through the maze of bureaucracy and paperwork to obtain full guardianship of your child, talk to other parents who have been through the process. Get good legal representation and keep fighting until you win. As much as you can, shield your child from the stress and chaos of the battle. Only share what they need to know and do your very best to make them feel safe and protected in your care as the process moves forward.

If you are fighting with their natural parents, try not to take it personally and don't say evil, judgmental things about them in front of your child. What you say about them may come back to haunt you in the very mouth of your adoptive child.

Finally, make sure you have a support group of friends and family who will weep with you as well as rejoice. In the journey of loving and rearing your adoptive child, you will have plenty of both experiences.

Chapter 4 - Safe Risks

Every morning, for several years, a little yellow bus had come to take Cetra to school. And each of those years I worried. I worried about her inability to navigate streets and landmarks. I worried about this false little cocoon that society built for children like Cetra. I wanted her to have freedom; to feel free and to have the right to choose whatever pathway her life might take. I knew that the days would come when there would be no little yellow bus waiting at the curbs of her life. Much of the time, she would be on foot in this life, and she would need to be able to trust the wisdom of past experiences and to remember what I had taught her about trusting God in dark days. As the years wore on, that little yellow bus became my enemy. It would have to go.

Graduation day from middle school was a happy day for Cetra and a joyous occasion for me. I watched my pretty little girl join the other children on stage to receive her certificate. I held back tears of relief and pride – I didn't want to embarrass her in front of her friends. Together, we had reached a huge milestone; but high school lay ahead. She and I talked about the new, giant step I needed her to take. I wanted her to walk to school each day rather than taking a bus. Although she agreed, I could see the fear in her eyes.

I moved two times looking for a home that would be close enough to her school so that she would not have a long distance to walk. On one occasion, I remember walking the distance with her. I can still remember how my heart trembled as the cars flew past her and the traffic lights and the visual assault of new, abandoned, and bustling businesses and buildings overwhelmed even me. This would not do. I had her name placed once again on the schedule for the little yellow bus, and I moved again.

Then, I made a decision that brought a turning point for both of us. I bought a beautiful little house that was only a few blocks from her high school. I moved into the main floor of the house, while she had the full run of the top floor where her bedroom was located. The huge backyard and the quaint manner in which each room opened up into the other were perfect for both of us.

As summer ended and her first big day in high school loomed ahead, I don't know what she was feeling, but I was a nervous wreck. Her first day sticks in my mind and heart and to think about it still brings tears. As all high schools are, this one was huge, bristling with activity and noise, and intimidating. I walked her to school that morning and promised to be there to walk her home when school ended. I wanted to give her all the time she needed to feel safe in walking the short distance alone. I sat through her homeroom class with her with a sinking feeling.

As the homeroom teacher gave each student their personal class schedules and a journal for students to customize their schedules, I was totally lost. With her learning disability, how would Cetra make her way from one class to the other? She still couldn't tell time or count money, and her sense of spatial direction and use of environmental cues were almost completely undeveloped. I feared the worse.

When it came time to leave, I turned to walk away and she grabbed my arm. I saw raw panic in her eyes and I almost lost it right in front of her classmates. She fell into my arms and held on to me for what seemed like dear life. I pleaded silently, "God, please help me...please help my child...please help both of us get through this moment and this day." And, He did in grand style. When I released her from my arms, her look of panic had given way to peace. I gave her one last reassuring squeeze and quickly made my exit.

After two days, Cetra was still unable to walk the short distance from our new house to her school. Although my stress level increased, the past shadow of the little yellow bus was gone forever. Somehow, the terror of those days were needed for both of us to move forward into a brand new day. We were going to get through this dilemma, I just didn't know how. Looking back, I am surprised at the things that seem obvious to me now, but through the lenses of worry and stress I could not see them. I now realize that there were entirely too many new things coming at her, as well as me. What I chalked up to her disability, no doubt was quite normal considering all of the new challenges that were occurring in her world all at once. What a thief and a liar fear is. It will distort reality in very grotesque ways.

Day after day we walked the route to and from school. Day after day she would get it wrong when I stepped back to let her take the lead. Why couldn't she get this? Although the route required several blocks of walking, there were only two turns – a left and a right and then a straight shot to the building. Each time, I carefully pointed out the landmarks that she was to watch for. The Rite Aid on one corner, the supermarket just across the street, and the gas station straight ahead. Still, she couldn't get it right. Even when we walked the route coming back home, she couldn't get it. The school building to her back, I explained to her, the long neighborhood of houses facing her would take her back to the Rite Aid, the supermarket and the gas station. Without fail, each time, she got it wrong.

We experienced the same level of difficulty with the combination lock I bought her for her locker at school. Just recently, I learned that children with developmental and learning disabilities may experience eye-hand coordination difficulties. This makes it difficult for them to discern right/left movements and this difficulty can be compounded by having to integrate combinations of numbers. Be that as it may, how soon we forget…years before, I had experienced the same frustration with my own gym locker! To assist her in overcoming this hurdle, I bought her a key lock with a smaller key so that she could distinguish her house key from the locker key. This seemed to work. Her teachers, unknown to me, had assigned a "buddy" to help her get to each of her classes. She never mentioned it, but I have learned that it is only when you stop worrying about a thing that you find out that things have a way of working out just fine.

The day finally came when I could not continue leaving work early to walk her back home. I went to a co-worker at my wit's end, but never for a moment did I think I had made a mistake in choosing the course we were on. Although I went to him to complain, he gave me the answer I needed to release my child into the liberty I so wanted her to know and enjoy. The lesson I was to learn is that even liberty, because it is so valuable, has a price that one should be willing to pay in order to lay hold of it.

As I whined on and on to my co-worker about how frustrating it was that she couldn't seem to get it, my friend sat there staring at me sympathetic but unmoved. His lack of expression bugged me. "Elaine," he started, "face the fact that the kid is going to get lost." This was out of the question. No way was I going to concede to the idea of my kid getting lost. Even as he spoke the words, my mind conjured up images of someone grabbing her from a dark alley, someone hitting her with their car and driving away, or worse still – her small form just walking and walking aimlessly in the wrong direction!

Patiently, he waited until my performance as Drama Queen of the Year subsided. When the curtain folded, I was emotionally drained, but also spent from worrying so much. The fight in me almost gone, I looked at him and asked how in the world his last words were so supposed to help me. That is when he shared with me a life-changing truth about what he called, "safe risks."

He explained to me that all parents go through what I was experiencing. Funny thing, I was only just now experiencing it because of the label placed on Cetra's life so early on. She had been imprisoned by psychologists, sociologists and a school board that felt she was incapable of achieving a thread-bare minimum. He then explained to me that parents operate on what they call a "safe risk" system. The safe risk system goes like this: There are some things that may be risky, but can be turned into safe risks if you prepare your child for the worse case scenario. A safe risk is not a risk that clearly places them in harm's way.

"Okay," he asked me, "are you ready to release her and allow her to get lost?" It was tough and it took me a while, but I finally wrapped my mind around it enough so that I could move beyond it. What next? "Next," he explained, "you must give her the guidance she will need so that she will not be in harm's way when she gets lost." How could I make this scary proposition safe for her? "Well," he explained, "you must make a decision about what you *don't* want her to do if she gets lost."

His logic was good and I decided to yield to the inevitable, without yielding my maternal instinct to take steps to ensure her safety. I didn't want her to knock on the doors of people's homes for help – that took care of the image of someone grabbing her and taking her hostage. I didn't want her to just keep walking and walking if she knew that she had lost her way. I wanted her to stop as soon as she realized she did not know where she was.

"Good, that's good," he encouraged. "Now, let's talk about what you would prefer to see her *do*," he continued. Recognizing what I did not want her to do helped me frame a different picture in my mind of her being lost that was not scary or life threatening. Well, I began, I would prefer that she asked other kids for directions that were leaving the school grounds and going in the same direction and that she felt safe approaching. I also preferred that she keep the building in sight so that she could go back to it if she was unsure if she were going in the right direction. If she could at least look up and see her school building from whichever direction she left, she could go back to it and get help from a teacher, hall monitor, or guidance counselor. In my estimation, these were "safe risks."

I sat with Cetra immediately and together we made a plan for the possibility that she might get lost. Her reluctance to accept the plan belied her relief in getting her nervous mother off her back. I had not a clue of how I had increased my child's stress level with my drama. To assure her, I promised that if I didn't hear from her within a reasonable amount of time, say 30 minutes, I would come immediately to the school and surroundings to look for her. She agreed that it was a good plan.

Well, the stressful day finally came. I instructed her that as soon as she arrived at our home from school she was not to even put her book bag down without calling me first to let me know she was home safe. At 3 p.m. on the first day and almost to the minute, she called me at work to say she had arrived home safe. The next day, the same thing occurred. She was home promptly at 3 p.m. Day after day, the calls came promptly around 3 p.m. – some days there was a slight delay of a few minutes which was absolutely allowed, but never more than 15 minutes after the hour.

One night at dinner at her favorite restaurant, I told her how proud I was that she had not gotten lost one single solitary day! The look in her eyes was unmistakable. Oh! Oh! Just as I was about to place my drama queen crown on my head with scepter in hand, a voice from inside rebuked me – almost kicked me. *Calm down*, I could hear, *calm down and just listen.* I took a deep breath and tried to recapture her gaze – she had dropped her eyes completely and was staring at a spot in the middle of her plate. "Cee," I started slowly, "what's wrong?" She looked up slowly and tested my eyes and facial expression looking for any sign of impending punishment. I deliberately softened my face and smiled at her. "Well, ma," she responded faltering, "I did get lost one day." Her next words almost drove me to tears. "*But*," she said calmly, "*I found my way home.*"

Over the years that would follow, there would be many other "safe risks" that she and I would have to take together, including her first bus ride alone into the city. But you know what? She never once got locked out of the house. She rarely arrived late to school or was late returning home. And, she has never, ever been lost – because no matter how many times you may lose your way in life, whenever you can find your way back home, "lost" is a concept that describes where you used to be and not where you are right now. ♪

Inspiration & Hope

Children with disability labels may be overprotected to the point of benevolent harm. In my own opinion, they will begin to live down to the standards lowered for them. If you, as the parent, fail to raise reasonable standards for what they can become in life, do not be surprised that nobody else will raise them either. As a community of parents, I think sometimes we look too much to non-familial caretakers to know what is best for our children. Then, we blame them when our child is stunted because of faulty assessments or misapplied theory. The fact is, these caretakers are trained to do a certain job and play a specific role in your child's life. To a certain extent, they can only perform their task well, if as parents, we remember not to abdicate our role as parents and the ultimate decision-makers.

Specialists and psychologists can provide guidance and support, but they should never be given the last word.

Taking risks with your child does not mean placing them in harm's way or pushing them to accomplish objectives that would be frightful or intimidating for any child. Work with your child and your child's specialists to determine the next steps your child is ready to take. They should be steps that are doable and reachable – for your child. Remember too that the disabilities in your child's life will play out as real impediments and should always be a part of the equation in terms of how high you raise standards for them. You should never raise a standard for your child based on how well you were able to do something when you were their age.

Finally, bear in mind that you don't have a disabled child, you have a child who has a disability. Examine the disability for what it is, test it, understand it, and help your child see it as a challenge that can be overcome, rather than a curse that is crippling.

Chapter 5 - Dolls, Dolls, Everywhere

One year my mom called me to ask if Cetra realized that she'd left two of her favorite dolls behind in Baltimore after summer vacation. Each year, I took her for an annual summer stay with my mother – I don't know which of us benefited from it more. I was surprised to hear this report because I had wondered the same thing when she'd left two of her favorite dolls with me at the beginning of the summer vacation.

My mother and I had the best belly-laugh ever as we talked about Cetra's tendency to forsake some of her dolls for others and play favorites with still others. Not all of them had names, but mom and I both knew what doll the other was referring to by description. Mom and I theorized that whenever she got tired of any particular doll, she'd leave it some place safe knowing that she'd eventually return for it when she was ready to pick it up again. As I chuckled with my mom over Cetra's funny idiosyncrasies with her dolls, the thought passed my mind that I'd better not let this kid decide where I'd spend my senior years.

Several years before, I'd been alarmed by the revelation that when Cetra had been taken by Child Protective Services, she had not been allowed to return to her home to retrieve any of her toys and books. On the day she was taken into governmental custody, she was turned over to a foster family with only the clothes on her back. She had not been afforded the opportunity to see or even speak to her custodial parent one final time. What thoughts of terror and abandonment must have plagued the mind of this eight year old child when she was taken into custody?

When I traveled to take custody of my Cetra, they handed her over to me with a small sum of money, a beat up suitcase containing a toothbrush, a pair of underwear, and a cheap pair of sneakers that can be purchased in the sales bins of stores like Rite Aid. I tried to turn off the visual images of the horrors that had brought this child to this point in her short days on this earth.

She always needed a doll with her everywhere we went. When we traveled to public places, I refused to allow her to take one with her. Although she was a tiny little thing when I gained custody of her at 10 years old, in my mind she was still too big to carry dolls around.

She kept several of them in bed with her when she slept at night. They'd be under her, around her, on top of her, and behind her. Some were teddy bears, some were stuffed dolls, and some were those carved-in-durable-plastic dolls whose eyes rolled closed when you moved them and whose tiny little faces were chiseled into hard smiles. I guess this is why they can get away with calling them dolls.

Until the day she left my home and life, I never fully grasped what dolls meant to her or what their presence provided in her life. What I do know is that on the day she left my life, she left every single one of them behind. Perhaps she left them because she was tired of them and believed she no longer needed them. It is my private hope and burden that she left them knowing that they were in a safe place to which one day she herself could return. ♪

Inspiration & Hope

Children may attach themselves to things as a way of having something through which they can begin to express their own unique identity. (Their attachment may also be an expression of their fear.) If you want to test this theory, just try taking a baby bottle or favorite security blanket from a ten-month old.

When you are dealing with an older child who has been through any kind of abuse, this seeming unhealthy attachment can be easily misunderstood. Don't be so quick to break what you consider a bad habit. Test it to see if it will run its course. If, in fact, the attachment is unhealthy, search for the root of the need it serves for your child. If you break the habit without understanding the longing, as they grow older, they will trade one bad habit for another.

To find the root of a longing, get into the habit of talking and listening to your child about that habit and without judgment or ridicule.

Chapter 6 - They Are Never Truly Yours

Cetra, although she was my adoptive child, was my niece by blood. As such, I was in every respect a member of her family. Imagine how I felt when she would express an obsessive longing for her "family" as if I were a stranger. I suppose that adoptive parents who have no such blood connection have it the worse.

I remember years ago being in a heated argument with a woman over the question of how an adoptive mother feels toward a child which is not her own. The grand proclamation was that you could never feel the same parental sentiment toward an adoptive child as you would your very own. Intuitively, I knew this statement was untrue, but I couldn't put forth an argument that seemed to work. All of these years later, the memory of that discussion moves me at an emotional level. Although I never bore Cetra in my body, had she ever been attached to my umbilical cord, it is impossible that I could have loved her more.

Doctors would remind me of this when they would ask for details concerning her early medical history. Teachers would remind me of this when they would inquire as to the pattern of her learning disabilities. Old friends would remind me of this when they recalled the fight I fought in trying to get her warden state to consider me a potential custodial parent.

I remember the early days when I was first awarded custody. My friends and acquaintances who knew that I had borne no children of my own, upon meeting Cetra would refer to me as her "Aunt." Funny little Cetra would get beside herself and correct them immediately with, *"she's not my Aunt, she's my Mom!"* In private, I had to constantly scold her about rebuking adults in this way. The memory tickles me now – it was as if she felt the need to protect my honor as her new Momma.

Sometimes, she would consciously acknowledge the period of her life of which I was not a part by raising questions about her deceased brother, or on rare occasions, questions about her natural parents. At other times she would amaze me with her stubborn unwillingness to admit that I was not who she claimed I was. It was at these startling times, that I realized the bond between us had transcended any concept of adoption – for both of us, we were as much a mother and a daughter as the sun was the counterpart to the moon.

As she got older, this changed. Perhaps it was the aging process that brought the change, or perhaps environmental issues like her friends, her books or what she watched on T.V. The day came when she became obsessed about going back to live with her "family." I can't say it was a sudden thing, but it did seem to come from out of nowhere. At first, it was just a reminiscing about her cousins, her grandparents, and her aunts. She could remember their names long after the point that she should have forgotten them. She would have been a very small child when she last saw them, and it is doubtful that they would have had a great deal of contact with her when she was so young. Nonetheless, she could enumerate their odd country names with efficiency and speed – all you had to do was ask. She could even differentiate cousin from aunt, although to me there seemed to be hundreds of them.

Gradually, her talk became a longing that I could not understand. These people had absented themselves from her life a long, long time ago and by choice. She would often talk of going back to live with them as if her life with me, her grandparents, her father, and her cousin and aunt on her paternal side did not count as "family." Although this tendency of hers to speak of us in this way did not hurt me, it certainly annoyed me.

One memorable event sticks out in my mind, but gave me pause for deep reflection. One Saturday morning, one of these relatives called my home after a silence of many years. She seemed unaware of the fact that Cetra had come into my care hating with all the vengeance that a ten year old could muster up. Rather than asking to speak to me first, she spoke directly to Cetra. Suffice it to say that I was not pleased. Evidently, she felt that her blood rights superseded my parental rights. After we exchanged very unpleasant words, and I made it clear to her what the rules of engagement would be, we seemed to be able to deal with each other on better footing. I agreed to allow her to send Cetra a family photo album of all of her cousins, aunts and other members of the extended family. What a mistake that turned out to be.

I knew that there was going to be a problem on the day the package containing the album arrived. In it, was a huge photo album including an 8 1/2 x 11, framed photo of one of her birth parents. There was also a letter and several other small objects including a long belated birthday gift. As we opened the package together and examined the contents, she snatched up the photo album and ignored the other items. This intrigued me. She immediately ran upstairs to her bedroom and closed her door. Although it was an emotional moment for both of us, intuitively I understood that I needed to release her to just go with whatever she was feeling – and that it was okay to do this, with or without me. It wasn't easy for me – but she wasn't a kid anymore. In addition, she had been steadily closing a wall around us, and redefining my role in her life. It had never been an outward, disrespectful challenge to my authority as her parent, but it was something much more subtle and imperceptible. She got to the point where she shared less of her feelings and her thoughts with me.

I gave her the privacy that she clearly wanted to view the photographs for herself. I felt left out and wanted her to share whatever this was she was experiencing with me. But I also knew that to demand inclusion would be unfair and selfish on my part. I decided to do the adult thing and allow her to share what she chose about her "family." Later that evening, I took the other articles up to her and reminded her to read them as I felt that much thought had been given about their selection. I marveled at how pretty the gift of jewelry was, and with a cautious addendum offered that I felt that Cetra resembled her birth parent a lot. She rankled at this, but said nothing. As I peered at her, she seemed completely absorbed by all of the faces in the album, and excluded me with her silence.

The next morning, she was late coming down to school. Cetra was never late leaving for school! I was alarmed when I realized that she had not yet left the house. When I called to her, she came bounding down the stairs and apologized with the explanation that she was looking at the photo album. When she left out of the house, I went up to her bedroom and was amazed to see all of the items from the package on her bureau unopened and un-inspected. The photo album was on her bed, but the picture of her parent was turned face down on one of the lower shelves of her entertainment center. I lifted it up and set it upright on her bureau, but Cetra did not let it stay there for long. Knowing Cetra as I did, the facedown photo of her birthparent left on the bottom shelf, spoke volumes. I did not find the jewelry sent to her until she had left my home a few months later – hidden in a corner in one of the bottom drawers still in its case, and untouched. The framed photo of her parent ended up discarded in a stack of old school papers and tattered magazines.

Eventually, that photo album had to go. She became obsessed with it to the point that she would carry it around with her everywhere in the house. She would sleep with it and spend her waking moments staring at one photo to the next. When it got to the point that she would lose track of time and would leave home late for school, I knew that I had to do something about that photo album. One night while she was asleep, I went up and retrieved it and hid it in my bedroom downstairs. The next morning, when I called her because she had not come downstairs to leave for school, I was startled to look up to see her forlorn shadow in the doorway to my bedroom. *"My photo album is missing Mom, do you have it?"* The alarm and panic in her voice troubled me deeply. It was then that I sat her down and had the heart-to-heart talk with her that probably I should have had days before. This thing with the photo album had gotten way out of hand.

We had many talks about her "family" after that episode and we determined between us that she needed to strike a healthy balance. She never did strike that healthy balance. While I confess to not truly understanding her obsession with the other side of her family which had never felt Cetra's birthday warranted even the conveyance of a Hallmark greeting card, I certainly understood her need to reconnect to them at some level. What I learned in the end is that no matter how much of your own heart you give away to them, they are never truly yours, and there is really no way to guard your heart against the impending rejection. The bloodline between natural parents and their seed is quite strong and endures the toughest emotion imaginable – even hatred – which is the fruit of abuse. ♪

Inspiration & Hope

At some level, all adoptive parents must face the pain of rejection and even abandonment. What I have learned is that your adoptive child is not making a conscious choice to reject you. What you are in fact experiencing is the residual effect of a whole range of emotional choices that they are trying to navigate with respect to their natural parents. What a mistake to feel that because your child appears to have an allegiance to their natural parents, they are somehow demonstrating a rejection toward you. It is not that simple for them, nor is it that black and white. If you would be honest with yourself, how many things in life are that simple? Any and all relationships that we have with people with whom we have soul ties tend to be very complicated, layered, irrational, dysfunctional, and even convoluted. Loyalty and love can seldom be placed in neat rational categories that make sense.

Make sure that you sort through your own feelings of anger and rejection that you may feel toward the natural parents, so that you don't drive your child to make choices that as children they are ill-equipped to make. Telling yourself that you don't have any feelings toward the natural parents doesn't even make sense. If you didn't feel *something* toward them, you would never have agreed with Child Protective Services to take the child into your custody.

Finally, the adage, "the grass always looks greener on the other side" is quite true. Just because your child thinks they would be happier living with their natural parents does not mean you should just hand back guardianship rights. People can change and become better; but most people who abuse children never get the help they really need. Ever.

Chapter 7 - Eating in the Basement With Dogs

When the New York State caseworker came to do a placement assessment of my home, her manner both insulted me and angered me. I was sure that I'd failed her evaluation. Mostly, it was her bluntness and her invasive manner that put me off. I wondered to myself who she thought she was talking to. I was not a welfare cheat or some poor, young mother with a bunch of children trying to get over on the "system." In my mind, clearly this was whom she came thinking she would have to deal with.

I was not the one who had failed Cetra and placed her in harm's way. I was her aunt, not one of her birth parents. The caseworker was talking to me as if I had been part of the abuse done to Cetra by numerous adults who had been charged with her care. I didn't know it then, but I was informed later that the caseworker had been instructed to deal with me in this manner. She knew a great deal about Cetra's beatings and abuse, and in collaboration with the warden state was looking to see if I could handle the emotional baggage that would accompany Cetra's placement. This encounter was to put me to the test, I learned.

After drilling me and insulting me, the caseworker switched gears and stated that she wanted to share some information about Cetra that I needed to have as a guardian parent. She then disclosed confidential information about Cetra's early abuse that left me numb just hearing it. Detail after detail poured forth from the records she peered at as she spoke to me. At one point, I wanted to snatch the files out of her hands and burn them. On and on she went, placing one indignity of abuse upon another. Finally, I could hear no more. I asked her to stop. The terror of what Cetra had suffered at the hands of human beings who had been her caretakers completely unnerved me. I was grateful that this dreadful encounter with the caseworker was over, and I wanted her to leave my home. I felt that I had totally flunked the assessment, which made me feel the more miserable.

When she left, I teetered emotionally between wanting to run and wanting to scream. In the end, I decided upon the former. There was a city park located close to my home at that time, so I went there and ran for a while and cried for a while. I ran because I didn't know what else to do with the pent up energy that wanted to burst forth upon the world. I cried for Cetra because I considered it a huge injustice that a child had to undergo such torment in so few years on this earth. Good Lord, the majority of this child's journey here, had been filled with torture.

At that moment, there was no thought of myself, nor how I would find the strength to parent her. At that moment, all I could think of was getting this bruised little angel into a warm home filled with safety and love. I wanted somehow to prove to her that what she had seen of life was not all that there was or could be.

When I was finally awarded custody of Cetra, I was equally taken aback by the stories of abuse and beatings that she had to tell from her viewpoint as victim. There was one recounting, however, that really shook me more than any other.

She shared about how one of her former foster parents would send her to the basement to eat with the dogs. She was such a tiny, under-developed little thing, that the image of her in somebody's dirty basement eating with dogs sickened me. I dared not probe for the how or when concerning these despicable episodes. I had read about people like her foster mother in books and even seen them handcuffed on their way to jail, but to have to face the reality of their existence in this world, troubled my soul. I just thanked God in spite of it all, because I knew that as bad as Cetra's reports were, they could have been worse.

You may ask how in the world it could have been worse. A few years ago, like many New Yorkers, I was watching the evening news report about how an imprisoned drug addict had left her two young sons in the custodial care of her drug addict sister. They were all barely existing in an abandoned building. When the police finally found the two boys in the basement tied to a filthy, feces-stained mattress, one was dead and the other emaciated and half-dead too.

The one who lived was taken into protective custody, cleaned up and fed. The other was buried having lived his few tender days on this earth in squalor and the worst of human degradation.

The one who lived would hopefully live out the balance of his days in love, but would he ever know peace in the secret of his soul and memories? Yes, Cetra had survived something closely similar to what these two young boys had faced, and she would get another chance at life if I had anything to do with it. What Cetra had been through was bad, but it could have been worse by many degrees. ♪

 *Inspiration & Hope*

Although I am not completely clear about why the secrets of a child's abuse must be protected, in a sense the cover-up can cause major problems for everybody involved. As the adoptive parent, you will hear about most of them anyway from your child, but there will be other details that will be shrouded in secrecy. These, you will hear about once your child is older and can look back at what has occurred to them from a more adult perspective. Unfortunately, the effects of the darkest of these secrets you may have to deal with in terms of their childhood behaviors and fears.

If your adoptive child acts out in extremely unreasonable ways, and exhibits mental and emotional torment, it is a sure sign that there is inhumane abuse behind it somewhere. When your child acts up in very chaotic and unruly ways that leave you baffled, you should always ask yourself the question, "What is my child trying to communicate with this behavior?" Most likely, the root cause of the behavior stems from torture that was inflicted upon them at the hands of early adult caretakers, including perhaps their natural parents.

Initially, the knowledge of what Cetra had been through crippled me emotionally. Just the details of it made me feel that I was ill-equipped to parent her. I became fearful for her and overprotective. This increased the stress in both of our lives and affected my ability to make sound choices for her.

You can never undo the injustices done to your child, but you can give them a new chance at life, and introduce them to a perspective of life that is both healthy and balanced. This you can do with love, stability, compassion and a forgiving spirit.

Chapter 8 - Tupac

When Tupac Shakur died from fatal gangland gunshots, I, along with numerous other parents all over America was mystified to discover that my child refused to accept the reality of his death.

There were more conjectures surrounding what *really* happened to Tupac than the number of Elvis sightings in Vegas. I don't know how other parents felt, but the "Tupac is still alive" craze totally befuddled me. The man had been shot multiple times at close range by someone who clearly considered homicide their profession. Even if Tupac had, by some remote chance, survived the deadly barrage of gunfire, why would he fake his own death? The economics of faking your death when you earn multimillions of dollars in video and music sales don't make sense, not to mention the inconvenience of having to change your identity.

Cetra, like most children and oddly even some adults, had numerous theories that she advanced to me about his faked death. She voiced these with such passion and conviction that she was sometimes comical and sometimes outlandish. On many occasions she tried with feigned impatience to convince me that there was *no way* that he could have died in the gunfire. One of her theories was that he was hiding away somewhere in the world until it was safe to resurface. Another was that the whole shooting had been staged by his mother to throw the real would-be assassins off his trail, and that his mother had done this to save Tupac's life. I never knew if Cetra concocted these on her own, or if there was some collective warehouse of such Tupac-is-still-alive theories from which she withdrew basic components.

For the first several months, her interest in the Tupac shooting was almost comical. She was such a funny little thing when she got animated and worked up. When it got to be six to eight months later, however, none of it was funny to me anymore. Her obsession with this dead, gangster rapper began to gnaw at me.

Elaine Rose Penn

I discovered that she would spend hours on end surfing websites devoted to discussion about the meaning of his life. The urban language of these websites was laced with profanity and raw slang. The fact that she had secretly engrossed and absorbed herself in their obsessive rhetoric unnerved me. I began to fret that Cetra's natural and childish tendencies toward fantasy-play might provide ground that was too fertile for some dangerous potentialities.

On a whim, I decided to change my tactic of trying to convince *her* that Tupac really was dead. I found that in allowing her the freedom to talk out her rationalizations, and without ridicule, that she was able to grieve for the young dead idol that she, like other children across America, wanted so badly to relate to.

Although I strongly disapproved of her choice for a hero, like most parents, I ultimately found that I did not know much about this powerful, young dead leader. While the decadence and urban violence of his persona may have been deliberately staged to appeal to the urban young, underneath the tough "keeping it real" façade, was a deeply spiritual young man who had the call of God on his life terribly. When I studied the depth and breadth of his purpose and how vast and layered it potentially was, his lifestyle of self-appointed destruction took my breath away. The allure of his rebellious styling, his music and his rhymes seemed to me a pied piper drawing masses of confused children into his own abyss. He was searching for a way to be a philosophical gangster; our children were searching for an invincible hero who was faster than speeding bullets.

I think it took a little more than a year, but Cetra eventually got over her Tupac thing. The day would come when as I inquired about her newest theory of Tupac's death and apparent resurrection, she would shrug at me quizzically and ask why I was asking. ♪

 *Inspiration & Hope*

We all need heroes and people we can look up to. Children, who are imaginative and impressionable beings, are particularly susceptible. In a child's world, these heroes take the form of actors, sports figures, and popular musical artists. They can even be cartoon characters. Although their choices may surprise you, and even alarm you, go slow with your ridicule! Remember that you once had heroes too and the more unlike your parents they were, the more superhuman you thought them to be. Don't worry, most of these heroes will be replaced by still others as your child ages.

Don't neglect to lay down some ground rules for the collection of memorabilia, posters, jewelry and the like. Monitor what your child is being exposed to in their movie selections, television programs, and music. In other words, don't stick your head in the sand and treat their obsessions as unimportant. Teenagers and even young children tend to mimic the dress styles, language and physical quirks of their heroes. Just recently, a good friend called to ask me to pray for the family of a young boy who hung himself while play-acting the dashing exploits of one of his popular superheroes.

Finally, I am always shocked and a bit upset to learn that when these "heroes" are interviewed, they often report not allowing their own natural children to view the videos and movies they appear in. In other words, they don't care what your child watches and listens to – they are only concerned about their own.

Chapter 9 - Teasing: The Peculiar Domain of Children

Teasing and name-calling appear to be the peculiar domain of children. How many of us adults can say we got through childhood and adolescence without being teased? As is the lot of every parent who must assist their child through the most fragile stages of development and life, I constantly had to figure out a way to help my Cetra get through the malicious name-calling to which all children become victim. For me, it became one more senseless burden of abuse that my adopted child had to endure.

When she was younger, around twelve perhaps, she would come home from school on cold, wintry days without her hat. It was a cute little thing, I thought, red, with a long tassel with a girlish design around the middle part. I liked it, but with a non-committal frown she had her way of communicating that there was something about it that she did not like. No amount of fussing, however, would get her to divulge her awful secret. I tried everything to persuade her to remember to wear her hat whenever she left school to go outdoors, but without fail, each day she would return from school with her hat tucked into her backpack. I should have seen it as a red-flag, but I hadn't yet reached enough practice at parenting to interpret what turned out to be a very clear message.

It was by accident that I discovered the reason behind her refusal to comply with my demand that she make sure that her hat was on and fastened when she prepared to return home from school. I was visiting with one of her teachers one afternoon for a parent-teacher conference and Cetra happened to be standing there with me listening. Just as I was about to leave, I mentioned to her teacher that I was disturbed that Cetra always came home without her hat on. At this, Cetra dropped her head in shame and startled me by making the declaration, *"the kids tease me when I wear it. They call me a troll."* My heart fell and I had to blink back tears. Not only did I feel the anguish in her little soul as she uttered her terrible secret, but I felt the little girl in me rankle at the memory of how much teasing can define your sense of self-worth when you are only a kid.

When the teacher acknowledged that she had witnessed the teasing, I understood why Cetra had so easily confessed it. The teacher also shared with me that she had disciplined at least one student for teasing Cetra and was on the watch for any others who were participating as well. Cetra looked up at her, and in a small plaintive voice stated flatly that there were others. Both the teacher and I in chorus admonished her to tell us whenever this occurred so that we could put an end to it. Her teacher reassured her that the behavior was mean and unacceptable, and that as her teacher she wanted to stop it from happening.

Of course, the red hat became a cursed thing with me. It had to go immediately. As a parent, I had not yet learned that when kids tease other kids, the act of ridicule is not about the disability per se, or the fact that you have big feet, or that your ears stick out funny from your head, or that your hair lays funny on your head, or even that you are overweight, skinny, or that your skin color is blue-black. It has more to do with children not being socialized to the point where they celebrate and respect the uniqueness of being human. As such, uniqueness in their mind too often equates to something that is weird and must therefore be satirized. I am convinced that as a society of adults who are responsible for the socialization of our young, we make it worse by endorsing this tendency toward mean-spirited satire. In my opinion, when it involves people -young, old, or disabled, it is little more than torment that leaves scars in the victim's soul.

As I raised Cetra from childhood to young adulthood, I fought a continuous battle to protect her from the teasing of her peers. Her developmental and learning disabilities often made her an easy and noticeable target. Her eccentricities would beg hurtful attention and other children would take advantage of the opportunity to laugh at the seeming abnormalities. I found that my never-ending battle to convince her that what the other children said was untrue, was largely a futile struggle. I'm sure that she learned – as most children do – to tease others as a means of avoiding it herself. I would like to think ideally, that in her aging process she also learned that just because somebody calls you a name that is not yours by birth, does not mean that what they call you, is who you are.

Just like most people, I enjoy the special gifting that comics have to make us laugh at ourselves, at life, and even the irrationality of others. I find too often, however, that more and more, the object of their material is aimed at the vulnerable, the defeated, the victimized, and the mistreated. If, as a society, we insist upon laughing at the demoralized as a means of relieving stress, than what we are left with is desensitization in the face of the most pitiable of the human condition. Children learn very quickly from example, and unfortunately ridicule is one they pick up and use rather quickly and against each other. ♪

Inspiration & Hope

As an adoptive parent, make sure you are fully apprised of the nicknames, labels, and disabilities that people have used to taunt your child. Never use these when you address or rib your adoptive child. They are neither funny, nor are they true.

Don't allow other children in the home to tease each other. Nip it in the bud immediately, and teach your child that respect begins by addressing an individual by the name they prefer to be called.

Chapter 10 - A Parent's Dream

If you ask anybody who knew Cetra – child or adult – what they will remember most about her, without pause, is the visual image of her always having a book in her hand.

This kid would read like some kids love to eat. From the day I took care and custody of her until the day I released her to her birth mother, she had a book close by. Her teachers shared with me that she would even walk down the halls at school with a book stuck in her face. They would ask her to please look up long enough to see where she was going. My sister and other friends would tell me that whenever she came around their kids with her books, she had a strange influence on them. They would get a book and start reading too!

When she was very young, I remember having to go to school to inquire about her performance in school. The teacher's chief complaint was that when the other students couldn't pronounce a word, instead of asking the teacher, they would turn and ask Cetra!! I had to try real hard that day to stifle a chuckle.

One of my chief complaints was not the money I constantly invested in her library of comic books and chapter books, but the fact that she insisted on reading out loud. You can imagine the stares I would get from other parents in the waiting rooms of doctor's offices. It took me years to break her of this habit, only to be replaced by another equally annoying habit.

Sometimes she would get so wrapped up in her reading that she would burst into laughter in restaurants, while riding in the car with me, at the home of a friend or anyplace else we happened to be. It was the one habit I was unsuccessful in breaking with her. I didn't want people to tease her about it or not understand it and think her strange. She had been teased enough for a lifetime.

Most often when I looked at her, I saw a mirror image of myself as a young girl. When I was a kid, I'd swallow up my loneliness in books. I'd traveled to far away countries in books, and I could disappear into the lives of pretty, popular girls who weren't born with skinny legs and too-big feet. Although the life I experienced in books may not have been the real world, it was a life that afforded me protection from early pregnancy, abortion, and drugs and street violence. It was a haven from the adolescent pull to grow up too soon.

I always knew that Cetra's love for reading was a huge blessing in both of our lives. Sure, she developed a wonderful vocabulary in the process, but she also gained an introduction to life that I could monitor, approve, and sanction as a parent. ♪

Inspiration & Hope

Sometimes as parents we become so focused on the annoying habits of our children, that we don't recognize and nurture their good habits. If your child is strong in any creative or intellectual ability, you need to give them lots of encouragement and praise. These might include a writing ability, playing a musical instrument, a gift of singing, a love for books, cooking, etc.

I remember that when one of my brothers was small, he would dissect every electrical appliance he could find. He seemed intrigued by wires, screws, and all of the other strange innards of electrical gadgets. Naturally, he drove everybody crazy – among other emotions. Today, he is an expert at electronics and security devices, and has owned his own businesses.

When I was a kid, I used to write on anything I could find – walls, mirrors, an old heating oil tank that had a blackboard surface, and occasionally, pads of paper. I loved pretending to be a teacher. Today, I consider myself a great trainer and no matter what else I find myself doing, there is an element of teaching in all of it.

When you see that your child has an ability or gifting in a certain area, recognize it, monitor it, direct it in healthy directions, and make an investment to perfect it. Years from now, your child may earn their livelihood from it.

Chapter 11 - Cetra, the Little Dictator

I suppose that we all have various shades of our personality that surface depending on the circumstance and even the climate of an experience. I never knew that such a demanding one was lurking just below Cetra's normally cooperative persona, until the day she had her wisdom teeth pulled out.

Although I still remember the whole episode with humor, I'd like to begin by recounting the most poignant part of it first. The removal of her teeth had been pretty routine, and thankfully there was no added trauma to the already stressful procedure. When the operation was done, the doctor called me into the post-op room to sit with her until the anesthesia could wear off so that I could take her home. When I walked into the recovery room and glanced at her still, small frame stretched out on the stretcher, my mother's heart did a somersault. She looked like such a helpless little thing with bloody-red wraps stuffed into her mouth, and her eyes in a constant roll. As I went over and took her hand, momentarily she glanced at me, but was too drowsy to make a real connection with me.

The nurse entered just behind me and walked up to her and kept calling her name. She responded with little gurgling sounds, but it was evident to both the nurse and I that she was not yet ready to be moved. From time to time she would moan and roll from one side to the other, and this would bother me a little. I didn't like the idea that she was in pain. I took a chair on the other side of the room because there was nothing closer, and pulled out a book to read.

Every few minutes the nurse would re-enter to call her name, but get the same response from my Cetra. After repeatedly doing this, finally she got more of a response on the fourth or fifth trip. As she took Cetra's hand and squeezed it gently, once again she called her by name. Cetra started suddenly, and partially sat up on the stretcher. She had a wild look in her eyes that caught my attention immediately. Her eyes darted away from the nurse and around the room as if she were terrified of something. I jumped immediately, but she met my glance as I approached her half way the distance between my chair and her bed. As soon as she caught my eyes, she locked her eyes with mine, and I saw something in her relax and her body once again went limp. What I saw was not just recognition, it was the look of a child desperately seeking her mother. "I'm here, babe, right here," I said to her as I gently stroked her hand. With that, she turned back again on her side and tried to go back to sleep.

Then, the other personality – the one I had never met before surfaced. She started trying to pull the bloody strips of gauze out of her mouth. The nurse immediately rebuked her. She explained to me that I was not to allow Cetra to do this because the action of pulling the gauze against the surgical wound would irritate it and cause it to bleed more. As she spoke this to me and to Cetra, what did my child do? She proceeded to spit the bloody strips out anyhow. As the nurse collected the strips, she amicably consented that perhaps clean strips would be more comfortable. She replaced the strips in Cetra's mouth, only to have her spit them out again seconds later. Was I going to have to swat my big 16-year old sick baby on the buttocks for being so difficult? Little did I know that this was just a taste of what I was going to encounter with this obstinate personality.

I managed to get her home and into bed with little trouble after the anesthesia had worn off pretty well. The first 24 hours were pretty interesting, to say the least. My mother and sister had driven in from Maryland to help me – she had always been their baby too, and this occasion was as notable an event in the Chronicles of Cetra for them as much as me. Adhering to the doctor's orders, I had purchased an assortment of yogurt and jello in many of her favorite flavors, as well as pudding and juices. As well, I had purchased lots of clean gauze to keep the wound dry and free of food debris. She was a good girl for perhaps the first few hours – as you may have guessed, she was asleep during that period.

After my family left and it was just she and I, things changed and she became a little dictator. My first mistake was to give her a little bell to ring when she needed me for anything because I didn't want her to stress the stitches in her mouth by yelling. And ring it she did. After about 2 days of it, I took it away and told her that I would check on her periodically to determine if she needed anything. My second mistake, which turned out to be a huge one, was agreeing to feed her in bed.

I would take her meals to her on a dinner tray and arrange everything just so. She would complain about the flavor, the brand, and my choice of selection. Because she was sick, it took all I could muster not to backhand her one good time. She would shake her head vigorously at my selections and cross her arms over her chest to indicate that she was not going to eat it. Changing the gauze in her mouth and getting her to take her medication, cooperatively, would take a story unto itself to describe. Like a two year old just learning to speak, she would look me squarely in the eyes and say "No!"

On about the fourth or fifth day when she was able to talk freely, she would yell for me to come to her, and I'm telling you more than once I thought seriously of doing her some harm. I would go up to her, hand on hip, eyes glaring, wondering what her main problem was. In as obstinate a voice as she could muster, with a surly look in her eyes, and through swollen still-tender gums, she would order me to get her something to eat with the added directive of telling me what she did *not* want. It was on about that fifth day that I had had it with Cetra, the little dictator. I announced that there was clearly nothing wrong with her feet or her hands and that if she wanted her meals in bed, she would have to get them herself. She seemed genuinely concerned that her servant had just quit.

I was so happy to send her back to school – you have no idea. Fortunate for her, that particular personality soon disappeared and I got my regular Cetra back. ♪

 *Inspiration & Hope*

Adopted children may act out in very problematic ways to become the center of your attention, even your affection. Some of them can be so starved for affection, that no matter how much you give, the more they seem to crave it. If you can see your child's insatiable need for your attention as a healthy, and very reasonable thing, you will most likely respond in healthy, adult ways. Gradually, the need for your attention will mature into other matters of need, but they will never completely abate. This is not a bad thing, if you seek to understand the root of what they are craving from you rather than the negativism of their behavior.

Practice being longsuffering; assure them of your love always; take time to listen to them; make your child a priority in your life.

Chapter 12 - Forgiveness

One of the things I miss the most about Cetra was her habit of turning on the outside porch light for me and greeting me at the garage door with a great big hug. Then she'd look at me with bright eyes that hid old mischief and ask, *"Mom, how was your day?"* After we'd exchange a barb or two, she'd turn on her heels and disappear into her bedroom on the top floor until dinner was served.

On this particular day, she changed her routine and I noticed it at once. Instead of disappearing at the top of the stairs, she followed me into my bedroom on the main floor chirping like a little sparrow. I can't even recall what she chattered about. When she was younger, I used to call her "my little chatterbox" because she was always talking and talking. She'd smile sometimes and say, *"Mom, I like it when you call me that."* On this day, she chattered non-stop and in a fog of tiredness I wondered what was up with her.

As she chirped on and on, absentmindedly, I hit the play button on my answering machine in my bedroom. I heard the voices of two women talking – one sounded vaguely familiar, but the other voice was unfamiliar to me completely. I sat down wearily to take my shoes off, and I overheard the voice that was familiar to me say the word "bitch." I stopped and sat up and turned in the direction of the phone unit. Cetra stopped talking and froze in one position. It was then that I noticed her face. I couldn't discern what the expression meant, but it was something akin to distress. Instead of turning toward the machine, which from what I could tell seemed to be the cause of her distress, she kept her eyes fixed on me. Very slowly, I stood and walked over to the machine and hit the play button again.

As I sat and focused my attention on the voices, Cetra never moved. She kept her eyes locked on mine. This time I could clearly hear the voices and with surprise recognized the identity of the familiar voice. It was Cetra talking to another woman who had a distinctly southern accent. The strange voice kept reassuring her, while Cetra complained about the "hell hole" she was currently living in. She told the strange voice that she couldn't wait to get away. It was then that I heard Cetra refer to me as a bitch.

The voices kept talking and talking, but I stopped hearing. This time, my eyes were locked on Cetra's. She turned from me slowly and walked toward the corner of my bedroom and stood there facing the wall. A voice screamed in my head, "don't say anything, get your keys and get out of the house." But I couldn't believe I just heard my child call me out of my name. I realized my mouth was hanging open and I turned to say something to the back of her head, but I heard the voice again. "Don't speak. Get your keys and get in your car and leave the house at once."

I grabbed my shoes and half running, half falling, I ran back out to the garage and got into my car and drove quickly away from my house. As I drove, tears welled up and spilled over, while my stomach started twisting in knots. I felt like a ball of fiery emotions. I was at once hurt, angry, in disbelief, and shock. I kept replaying the voices over and over again in my head. Had I heard what I thought I heard? Was this a bad dream?

As I drove through the streets, my thought was to get out and walk and walk and walk. The inner voice spoke to me again and said, "No. Go to a public place where there are a lot of people. Don't go anyplace alone." I pulled into my favorite ice cream stand and was at once overwhelmed by the sight and sound of families and couples gathered enjoying ice cream and frolicking with each other. It was a beautiful evening and a light breeze danced all around the merrymaking. I bought an ice cream cone and sat at a table that was smack dab in the middle of all of the noise.

To this day, I have no clear concept of how long I stayed there. I sat and sat. No more tears would come, but my heart ached. It was a throbbing pain that made my heart feel like it was going to burst. I remember feeling empty-headed as if no thought could rest with me for more than a second. Thoughts would enter and then run away in a haze. As I sat there numb, I glanced up momentarily and caught the gaze of a young man who sat several yards away just staring at me. He wouldn't relax his focus, but kept his eyes fixed on me. It bothered me and I felt exposed. Was he watching me to assault me? Did I look as vulnerable as I felt? I felt like he had somehow read my mind and knew my darkest secret. My child had referred to me, her mother, as a bitch. To get away from the strange attention of the young man, I stood and walked back to my car quickly and drove home.

When I got there, the house was dark and quiet. I went to my bedroom and changed quickly out of the clothing I'd worn to work that day. As I passed the darkened stairway leading up to my child's room, just for a moment I strained to hear a sound. There was none. Quietly, I fixed my attention on preparing dinner. I felt strangely exhausted and my movements were mechanical and emotionless. My usual manner was to call to her to set the table for dinner, but on this night, it seemed a pointless thing to do. Had we ever been a family, she and I? My own child had referred to me as a bitch and was planning to run away from me.

I was too tired to sleep and too tired to do anything else, so I just sat staring at my living room walls like a prisoner in my own emotions. About an hour or more passed when I heard her quiet footsteps descend the stairs. She came directly into the living room where I sat motionless and empty. I didn't even bother to look up at her. What would be the point?

Out of the corner of my eye, I watched her movements. Initially, she stood still staring at me as if she were afraid of a coming storm. She must have been mildly disappointed to see that there would be none, ever, over this issue. I felt as if something had entered the gates of my life and would forever remain fixated to this place and time. Then, she stood on her tiptoes and tipped slowly toward me until she stood directly in front of me. For the first time, I glanced up at her and looked directly into her eyes.

Her pain took my breath away. For a second my mother's heart screamed out, "grab her, take her into your arms, and make whatever is bad, good again." But, I couldn't move. Something leaden and heavy had me weighted to the sofa. It was internal and had managed to squeeze all of my strength away. Her eyes were pink and puffy where she'd cried and cried. What had my child suffered alone when I left my home? Perhaps she'd had to fight the fear that I would never return to her, or that I had left her like she'd been left by so many others. Had she punished herself for calling me that horrid word? What were the thoughts that had whirled around and around in her mind?

When she tried to speak, at first nothing would come out but a whisper. I sat looking up at her emotionless. I had nothing to offer and no thought of how I could assist her. My heart wept for what she was feeling at this moment, but I felt like I'd been beaten badly and was too wounded to even surrender. "*Mom*," she managed to get out in a shaky voice. For a moment I remembered that just hours before, she'd referred to me as a bitch to that voice on the machine. She seemed to muster up courage, and I could see her face and lips tremble as she said the next words that brought reconciliation to both of our hearts.

"*Mom*," she repeated, "*you may never trust me again, but you still have to forgive me.*" I leaped up from the sofa and she fell towards me. I grabbed her into my arms and we both wept together, our tears mixing and washing us both. We held on to each other tightly. I remembered how she'd come to me as an angry little girl who hated her birth parent and who seemed angry at the adult world for hurting and abusing her. Over the years, I'd fought her anger with love, and I'd taught her the language of forgiveness. At that moment, I thought about how badly she needed me to forgive her and release her. Although her words had caused me great harm that day, I thought about what a critical moment this was and how my response to her error would be the greatest lesson in forgiveness I'd ever give her or learn myself. ♪

Inspiration & Hope

Probably, this episode was the defining moment in the life's journey that Cetra and I took together.

When Cetra came to me, the toughest lesson I had to teach her was regarding the issue of forgiveness. Ultimately, I had to walk the talk myself. In forgiving her, I learned something about myself, and she learned that forgiving is as important a power as asking for forgiveness.

Chapter 13 – A Light At Dusk

There are a lot of things that I miss about my precious Cetra, but there are several things that are both poignant and funny that I would like to share with you.

One of the first things I miss in terms of physical changes was her habit of turning on the front porch light to my house at dusk. It's funny how you don't even notice these kinds of small contributions that children make to the world. I think too much that we parents focus so much on what we do for them that we usually don't stop to notice what they provide for us.

I didn't even notice this gift of hers to me until that first night that I drove home once she was no longer in my life. You know, there is always a first night alone, a first dinner eaten alone, a first of whatever, when a loved one is gone from your life. Well, on this first night alone, as I drove to my home after work one evening, I almost drove past my own house. To my consternation, I realized that the front porch light had not been turned on! It was then that it hit me that this was something Cetra did for me in deliberation and in thoughtfulness. I really miss that light in front of my house when I come home in the evenings. The absence of that light is always a reminder that she is no longer here to take care of me.

Once I would enter my home, the sound of my garage door was the signal she needed to turn down her boom-box. Aren't kids something? Do they really believe that us parents were never young? Then she would come bounding down into the kitchen with a bright-eyed look of innocence and charm, and she'd throw open her arms and say, *"Ma, give me a hug – I like hugs!"* And I'd grab her, though weary from my day, always wanting to take her into my arms to love her tightly, even as much as I needed her to hug me. Not being able to touch her and embrace her now is perhaps the hardest part of learning to live without her.

She used to get so exasperated with me when she would find me having a bad hair day or unable to decide on an outfit. She would switch roles and become the mother and say to me with more than ample impatience, *"Ma, you look fine! You're a cutie!"* On many occasions and to my delight, she would even exclaim that I looked like a teenager. At this, I could never manage to fully suppress a giggle. She knew just how to touch the something in me that needed special handling, and could always sense when I was uneasy or stressed.

The other thing I miss the most about her is the sweet and reverential way she would approach me when she was with me for a ministry engagement. I used to call her my little armorbearer. When I'd sit down and the hostess would serve me a glass of water, she would tip toward me and pull a shawl around my tired shoulders. Then, she would wrap it snuggly around me and pat it just so before looking me in the eyes to see if she'd done it right. I'd look up and meet her eyes always intrigued by her gentleness and sensitivity in carrying out this small, but important chore.

Later, when I'd get home, most of the time all I felt like doing was taking a hot shower and balling up on a comfortable chair in my living room – trying to come back down to earth. Without fail, I'd look up and find her tip-toeing into the room with a hot cup of lemon tea – with just the right amount of sugar and simmering at just the right temperature. She'd tip-toe in a few minutes later to ask if she fixed it the right way. She always did, but I'd smile at her anyway and say, *"Babe, its perfect!"*

Somehow, someway, she picked up the habit of being able to quite successfully mimic foreign accents and voices. She could carry on a whole conversation in one of these dialects! I would double over in laughter and sometimes beg her to do one for me on the spur of the moment. No matter how hard I tried, I could never get her to show off this talent for guests. To my amazement, she would always act as if she didn't know how to begin.

Along these lines, she had what I call *Famous Cetra Quotes*. One of them was, *Get over it!* Sometimes, things would absolutely flabbergast me and since she was the only guinea pig available, I would sit during these times and lay my issue out for her as if she were my counselor and judge. After listening intently, she'd finally tire of my circular reasoning, and say, *"Ma, I think you should just get over it!"* This of course, would reduce me to laughter, because usually she was right.

One of her other famous lines was, *"Dogs drool, cats rule!"* Just to egg her on, I'd always reverse it and say, *"Dogs rule, cats drool!"* She loved cats and hated dogs. It never failed that when she encountered one on her way to or from school, I had to hear about the hated experience. With much drama and fanfare, she would describe what the encounter was like and end with a threat of what she planned to do the next time she came across that dog!

I remember once when she was a little bitty thing of about 3 years old, we looked around to find her missing – she had gone outside to the backyard of my mother's house. Upon hearing the insistent barking of a dog, both my mother and I ran frantically toward her. We were soon reduced to laughter when we found her at the chain fence separating my mother's house from the neighbor's house stomping, yelling and pointing her little 3 year-old finger at the dog on the other side of the fence. Most little kids would have run in terror – but there she was deliberately aggravating the huge animal. And there he was, barking back at her with teeth barred, and for all he was worth.

"Ma, how'd I do?" was her other famous quote that I miss a lot. She always seemed to hunger for my approval and affirmation. She was not a perfect kid – no kid is. When I think of her, however, I really have to struggle to remember those times when she was a disappointment to me. What I remember most, and cherish most, were the sacred and funny little things that she did and said that made her the joy of my life. ♪

Inspiration & Hope

As your child ages, their personality will go through quirky maturation, and at a certain point, they may even become jaded about life. All of their funny little mannerisms and infamous quotes will one day disappear into the cool façade of teenage-hood. Later, as they struggle to navigate the disquieting waters of adulthood, they will forcefully carve out an identity separate from the one you have made for them since they came into your care.

You will never see this side of your child again, so enjoy as much of this stage of their life as you can, and savor each sacred – and funny – moment for all that it is worth.

Chapter 14 - Poogie Bear and a Doll Named Annie

The day that my heart dreaded for nearly a year had finally come. I knew a little more than a year before that I needed to release my daughter so that she could start her new life with the birth mother whom she had not seen for nearly twelve years. My heart wept and wept. How could I let her go? Although I had never carried her in my body, I had carried her in my life and heart.

The night before she would leave my life, she and I had carefully packed the last of her books and personal belongings. When we got to Poogie Bear and Annie, a shadow crossed her face and I lifted her chin to see if I could get her to tell me what was on her mind. These last few days that had been filled with good-byes, packing, and final long-glances, had worn on her emotionally. With a look of embarrassment, she spoke to me in a small voice and told me that she needed to have them with her in her bed that night. She was 18 years old.

I smiled at her quickly and turned away so that she would not be embarrassed further. I had never fully understood her obsessive need for stuffed animals. What I did discover was that when she was taken into custody as an abused little girl of eight years old, the courts had refused to allow her to return to her home for her toys, books or stuffed animals. She had never seemed to outgrow what I viewed as an unhealthy need to have several of them tucked into bed with her each night. Some nights I'd peer into her room and she'd have them tucked under her head and beside her body as if they were life preservers.

Her graduation ceremony was scheduled for the next morning, and her stress level had spiked as we both awaited news of what had happened to her birthmother and stepfather. They had been due to arrive in town by mid-day that day and had not as yet arrived. Would I have to console my child once more over yet another heartbreak associated with her natural parents – and of all occasions

– this one, which was her graduation day? To calm her, I wanted her beside me on our last night together. After tucking her in for the night, I reflected back on our years together.

I remember how painful it was to put the ministry backseat to anything or anybody, including this new child of mine. For the first year or so, I actually resented having to sacrifice the ministry for her needs. I loved the ministry passionately and it had always been my first love. As a single woman, it had always been my first choice above everything. This child of mine changed all of that. From the first day I gained custody of her, she had turned my world upside down.

I'll never forget the Saturday I rode with my former pastor, who was also my mentor, and his wife to the New York State fairgrounds. I was in the back seat crying all the way. My daughter had come to me as a bundle of problems, issues, and disabilities. She had been given the awful label of Slightly Retarded, and was pronounced by a team of specialists and school psychologists as never being able to have the capability of succeeding with other youth her age. I'd already moved twice in six months, trying to find the right school district, and even the right neighborhood to raise her in.

"Why didn't you tell me I would have to go through all of this in raising her?" I asked him tearfully. What Pastor Thomas said to me next, I have never forgotten, and over the years I have repeated constantly for other adoptive parents whose hearts bleed as well. He said to me, "Elaine, I knew that you would have a hard time raising the little girl. I know how much you love the ministry and how much it means to you. *I wanted the little girl to have a chance at life.* No matter what you confront in raising her, you will get through it. You are going to do just fine. One thing you need to settle right now, however, and that is that everything else must now take second place in your life."

I wept and wept. Putting anything before the ministry was tantamount to putting something else before God in my estimation.

I simply could not understand how or why anything should have prominence over the ministry. Had I made a mistake in adopting her? How could I ever come to love her to the extent that I stopped resenting her for needing so much of me as a mother?

It strikes me that there were two women named Mary and Martha in the Holy Scriptures who faced the same dilemma. May I show you a few things for your enlightenment? Let's look at this interesting portion of scripture from Luke 10:38-42,

> *"Now it came to pass, as they went, that he entered into a certain village: and a certain woman named Martha received him into her house. And she had a sister called Mary, which also sat at Jesus' feet, and heard his word. But Martha was cumbered about much serving, and came to him, and said, Lord, dost thou not care that my sister hath left me to serve alone? Bid her therefore that she help me. And Jesus answered and said unto her, Martha, Martha, thou art careful and troubled about many things: But one thing is needful; and Mary hath chosen that good part, which shall not be taken away from her."*

Like Martha, most of us women who carry the gospel and who are also wives and mothers develop some type of martyrdom complex as we rush about serving God at the expense of our marriage and the well-being of our children. I noticed a couple of other things about Martha, however, that I had never seen before. First, Martha wanted the Lord's attention real bad. You will notice that while serving the Lord and ministering to the Lord's needs, she stops and demands that Mary be required to help her. As I examined this closely, it occurred to me that had her motive really been one of service, she would not have really cared what Mary was doing. Further, I really do not believe she wanted Mary's help. What she wanted was for Jesus to give her the same amount of attention that he was giving Mary.

Please notice a few more things about Martha that entrapped her emotionally. She demonstrated a false sense of obligation to serve the needs of our Lord. Jesus rebuked her and pointed out that Mary had chosen a *good part* and he was not going to ask Mary to give this up just so she could be seen doing busy work for him. Interestingly enough, it is this false sense of obligation that is nothing more than a false belief that the world is going to collapse without the contribution we make.

I see something else in this revealing portrait of Martha. I see a woman who has misplaced priorities. She thought she was doing all of her work *for the Lord*. Jesus, who speaks as prophet in this interesting accounting, sees through to her real motive and characterizes her rushing and running about as being *cumbered by many things*. If our Lord were to assess what many of us say we are doing for his sake, I wonder how much of it he would dismiss as being *cumbered*? That word in the Greek is *perispao*, it means to *drag all about* or to be *distracted*. Can you imagine how Martha must have felt when our Lord characterized her service to him as being *dragged about*?

Now look at Mary for a moment. Mary is serving the Lord by being still. She is seated quietly at his feet and listening to his heartbeat. It would have been easy for her to feel a false sense of responsibility and sacrifice and to rush about with her sister. She wanted something more than just his approval. She wanted to know him and to learn of him – and she discovered that place at his feet. To find that place, she had to settle herself and not succumb to the pressure of thinking that *doing for Him* was the same as *pleasing Him*.

When my daughter came to me, she was a bruised and broken little girl. She needed a mommy a whole lot more than people needed another preacher. The greatest sacrifice I could make for the sake of the Kingdom of God was to be her mommy with my whole heart. She hadn't had a mommy for an awful long time and she needed my love, she needed a stable home, and she needed to know that no one would come and hurt her or take her away ever again.

I learned that she was the priority that God expected me to take care of first. I discovered that in loving her and serving her needs, I was truly serving the needs of the Church at large. To do so, I had to give up some speaking engagements and I had to do it with a willing heart. I had to make her my number one priority. I never wanted her to feel that this God whom she could not see was more concerned about His Church than her birthdays, her graduations, her sick days, her days of blossoming womanhood, and the pivotal, sacred moments of her life.

I have seen her through the most critical season of her life; and I taught her the language of forgiveness so that she could walk free of a tormented past. I wanted to show her that I am also a lady and a person who can make mistakes but ask for pardon. I wanted her to know a life of sit-down dinners, walking together just she and I hand-in-hand, mother and daughter chats that have been priceless, and times of great sadness and sorrow that we survived together.

As I reflect back on that day in late June of 2002, it occurs to me that serving my child has been *my good part*. That next afternoon after her birthparent's arrival and the climax of her graduation day, there was a mad hustle and bustle to get her personal belongings packed into her birthmother's car. I ran up to her bedroom to check it once more to make sure she had not forgotten anything. There, lying neatly on her pillow was the worn out and tattered bear named Poogie that used to be a hot pink, with one eye long-missing and the other cockeyed and hanging by a loose thread. Next to him was the stuffed doll named Annie which was a mongrel held together by one of her first baby dresses, and buttons for eyes, and a few strings of yarn still left over for hair.

Oh goodness, I thought, she has forgotten Poogie Bear and Annie! I ran out into the hallway and called to her from the top of the stairs.

She came running up the stairs and met me in the entrance of her bedroom. I half-laughed, half-smiled in a teasing way with Poogie Bear and Annie held up in my arms. "Um, you've forgotten these two somebodies, didn't you?" I held them out, expecting her to reach for them gratefully. Instead, she backed up, with her eyes locked on mine. "Mom," she declared, "I don't need them anymore." With that, she turned on her heels and ran back down the stairs, leaving me alone with Poogie and her doll named Annie.

For those of you who are mothers, you can pretty much imagine the surge of emotions which hit me all at once. I felt faint and had to sit to get myself together. I wept quietly alone, but not out of sorrow. I wept more from a mixed sense of accomplishment and melancholy. I was really losing my baby, and in more ways than one. In spite of this startling reality, I was reminded by this sweet and tender episode that the most important ministry assignment that I'd ever be given in my life was to serve the needs of my child fully and unselfishly. Not only did she not need Poogie and Annie anymore, she didn't need me anymore in the same way. With God's help, and the wonderful, enduring counsel of two wonderful people, I had helped Cetra become a whole, healthy young woman who had been given a *chance at life*. Mission accomplished.

I no longer have my Cetra, but I still have Poogie Bear and Annie to remind me that the greatest ministry I have ever provided to the world has been to my own child. They are still in the same spot where she left them as evidence that she no longer needs stuffed animals to feel safe in this world. ♪

Inspiration & Hope

The fact that you risked taking an abandoned child into your life means that you are a truly amazing human being. Although there will never be a ticker tape parade to honor you, medals awarded to commemorate your bravery, or great accolades pronounced for your mighty deeds, you are a hero just the same. Some give life; others save life, still others like you, are life preservers.

In case no one ever does, allow me to say, "Thank You for being such a great human being." As far as I am concerned, people like you are God's angels unawares.

Chapter 15 - One Fine Day

There were many sacred milestones in Cetra's life that I shall always remember and hold close to my heart. You know the ones I'm talking about – the kind that remind you of those old patchwork quilts that your grandmother made by hand. Remember how comforting they were pulled up around your neck on a cold winter morning? Cetra's graduation day from high school was just like that for me.

The drama that surrounded her special day was to be expected I suppose, but I could have certainly done without the tears that accompanied her day as well. That night before, she tossed and turned. Neither of us knew the whereabouts of her birthmother and stepfather who were on their way from their home state to celebrate this grand occasion with her. It would be the first time she would set eyes on her birthmother in twelve years. The only thing we knew was that they were on their way and should have arrived mid-day the day prior to graduation day. As night fell, they had not arrived and had not called. Cetra had been a bundle of nerves and I admit that my own were shot as well.

My own family had arrived on the day expected - these included her paternal grandmother, her father, her nephew and her aunt. Thank God for that extra day. My sister, brother and I used the opportunity to calm my mother who was not happy to see her grandbaby taken away by this estranged parent. We wanted this day to be special for Cetra and made a pact of peace for the entire weekend of celebration. This was Cetra's choice to return to her life with her birthmother and we had each faced our private fears and determined to release her. It was hard enough to let her go, and I had no space left in my emotions to handle anybody else's grief or fear. Somehow, someway, I had to let my baby walk out of my life, who knows – perhaps forever. I needed all the strength and resolve I could muster to get through this and to help my baby through this as well.

Well, as you suspected, her birthmother and other members of the family made it in the knick of time. I had driven Cetra ahead to the civic auditorium so that she could march in with the rest of her graduating class. When I returned home to direct my own family to the auditorium, I was greeted with the news that her birthmother and stepfather had called from the civic auditorium and had managed to ferret out Cetra for a glorious welcome and greeting. I had mixed emotions about all of this – none of it was going according to plan. They wanted to know if they could use my home for a quick change of clothing. I suppressed my feelings of being put upon – my goodness, this was my child's graduation day – did I have to go out of the way for somebody else on this day too?

Dutifully, I drove quickly back to the auditorium with my family in tow and directed Cetra's birthmother back to my home. After getting through the clamor of trying to get everyone seated, we finally all settled in the auditorium in what turned out to be some of the best seats in the house. You will not believe what happened next.

Everything was going smoothly. My family was to my left, Cetra's young stepbrother was to my right, and her birthmother was seated right next to him. I was choking back tears and trying to hold it all together as the principal called out the names of the graduates in alpha order. It was when they got to the "P's" that the next drama took me by surprise. Cetra's young stepbrother had to go to the bathroom and his mother did not want to miss Cetra's name being called for the acceptance of her diploma. She turned to me with a plea in her eyes and asked if I would please take her little boy to the bathroom. Initially, I was appalled. I felt trapped and wanted to yell at her "NO!" Something in me caved in when I saw the tears in her birthmother's eyes. My goodness, after all I had agreed to sacrifice in allowing my child to walk out of my life, would I have to sacrifice this moment too?

Although the request was not fair, it occurred to me that this woman had not a clue of who I was. During the crucial years of Cetra's life, I had been the woman that Cetra had addressed as

"Mom." Clearly, this woman, who was undeniably her birthmother, had assigned herself some special but undeserved status in my daughter's life. In my mind, her role had been an afterthought and not a central consideration. Clearly, it never dawned on her that I had more right to cherish this day with the child she had given life to than she ever would. Perhaps there would be other days and other special moments that she could claim as belonging to her and Cetra alone, but not this one. Selfishly, I felt that this day should belong to just me and my child and everyone else could come by invitation only.

Momentarily, I looked at her eyes filled with pain and thought of the private tears I had shed through the years with guidance counselors, teachers, and even the children who sometimes teased my Cetra. Where had she been through those years? Had she cried my tears or felt the anguish that all parents feel? What right had she to ask for this gift?

You guessed it – I mustered up all the grace and compassion I could and took the little boy to the bathroom. As I pushed through the standing-room only crowd to find the ladies room, I did not rush. It occurred to me that although I might miss the sight of my baby receiving that diploma in hand, I had already been her biggest celebrant for ten critical years of her life. Nothing and no one could bruise my heart on this day – it was Cetra's special day and as far as I was concerned, the pomp and ceremony was just the dessert – I had traveled the main course with her for ten wonderful years.

When I got back to my seat and managed to still my heart, my mom and sister smiled at me and whispered that they still had not gotten to Cetra's name!!! Glorious! When they did, they actually pronounced her first name correctly. She and I in private adulation and great joy leaped a wonderful jig. In her many years of secondary schooling, her teachers and counselors were always mispronouncing her first name. They would mispronounce it as *Setra*, instead of *"Cee-tra"* and it would get her goat every time! Today they got it right, but I imagined to myself that they had probably been set straight by her so many times that they couldn't have gotten it wrong had they tried.

She had made it! She had gotten through graduation day with her family all around her. What must she have felt to have both of her birthparents with her on this day? We did not have the opportunity to sort it out and discuss it privately between ourselves, but oh my I sure wish I had. She was such a funny little thing even at 18 years old, and could say some things that made you laugh and laugh.

On that fine day some two hours after her graduation, I had to say farewell to my wonderful, sweet Cetra. Her birthmother and stepfather needed to return home quickly and I had to leave for a trip myself that same day. We all agreed to return to my home for quick clothing changes and to pack Cetra's things into her birthparents' car. The balance of her things had already been shipped to her new home.

The plan was that we would all go celebrate this day with Cetra over dinner and say our final goodbyes at the restaurant. My God, could you please help me get through this last thing that was so filled with melancholy, finality, and an achy something that was hard to define. When we all got there, the maître d' led us to a table. To my surprise, Cetra's birthmother maneuvered Cetra and her own family to a different table in an adjacent section of the restaurant. To hide my hurt and disappointment at this turn of events, I focused on my mother's unbridled feelings of offense. After all, this was Cetra's day and we'd all come together specifically to laugh and celebrate her accomplishment. As my sister and I tried to make it better for my mother, I quite frankly did not know how to feel. Should I object to this? One part of me wanted to have a showdown with her birthmother but the other part of me knew that I needed to let go. The inner struggle mixed with pain was incredible. *Lord, just please help me get through this*, I prayed.

Of course, I understood what her birthmother was trying to do, I think. Evidently the plan was to make this as painless for Cetra as possible. Still, secretly, I resented her just taking over and beginning to make decisions about my child without checking with me first. This day was still mine as a parent, even if it would be my last.

Somehow we got through dinner – it was strained and no one was happy at my table. We tried not to show it, but the air was stiff with disappointment. We didn't say much, and it was hard to enjoy the food. I think each of us ate something, but I also remember a lot of wasted food left on our plates. The moment had finally come to leave; we could find no other excuse to linger behind.

I got up first from my place and my family followed. I felt like I was walking the plank. I determined to do this for Cetra and not for her birthmother – this day was still our day and I wanted to cherish whatever I could take just for me and her alone. I went directly to her and kissed her on her cheek, looking straight into her eyes I whispered, "babe, I love you" and I walked away and out of the restaurant quickly. My family followed my example, and just that quickly it was over and done with. I walked out of Cetra's life that day in great anguish, not knowing but caring deeply about what might befall her in the days and years ahead.

There are many emotions that still linger around my heart that are forever connected to that day and that occasion. It was a day that both Cetra and I had looked forward to with great joy and it was absolutely wondrous – filled with new beginnings, old shadows and questions, fear, tension, love, celebration, and pain as well. I'd seen her through many valleys and some mountains that tried to stand in her way, and had been given the great pleasure of seeing her cross that stage to accept her high school diploma. When she turned the tassel on her cap and grinned with her broad Cetra-smile, I had one thought in my mind and that was – "Thank you Lord, with your help, we made it!" What a fine day it was. ♪

 *Inspiration & Hope*

I began preparing for Cetra's leaving at least a year before her graduation day. We had many talks about her decision to return to her birthmother. This means, I had time to embrace the idea of releasing her. If your child ever leaves you under these circumstances, the most precious gift you can give them is to release them with poise and grace. The less drama and negativism that surrounds their departure, the more likely they will call you if their life ever depends on it.

I found that releasing someone you love is perhaps the most difficult task there is in life no matter what the circumstances. It is, however, possible and essential. Release is not the same as death, however; and a goodbye does not necessarily mean fare-thee-well forever.

Chapter 16 - Letting Go is a Process

Cetra had only been gone for a few weeks and the terror of not knowing how she was doing with her new parents and her new surroundings was really beginning to take its toll on me. Thank goodness for the countless faces in elevators and hallways at work who just let me talk and ramble on and on about missing her. Many of these faces were parents of adult children who themselves had been through this painful process. They knew how I felt and knew that there were no answers to give. Their compassion and their liberal willingness to just listen helped me through one of the most difficult times in my life.

I quite frankly did not know how to let Cetra go. Each time I thought of her, my heart squeezed and squeezed until I found myself a bundle of tears and unrelenting emotion. The smallest things reminded me of her and whenever I was in the company of other teens who were her friends, I would see her face in theirs. There were some restaurants that were our favorite hangouts that I could no longer even visit. How in the world could I get through this maze of grief?

I rarely ever went up to her bedroom, but one day I found myself at the top of the stairs wandering through her small former space like a lost child myself. Her room was a beautiful purple – when we'd move into the house, she insisted that her room be painted her favorite color. I'd even painted the downstairs landing the same color. Now, with her gone, it was wearisome to me.

The room itself was largely unchanged, except that most of her personal things were gone. Still, there were a few old toys and mementoes that she'd left behind, along with an assortment of books. As I aimlessly moved from one spot in the room to the other, I picked up an old school yearbook with her name on the cover. It read *Cetra Rose Penn*. My initial reaction was to smile at the memory of her taking my middle name and adding it to her own.

But then, the smile quickly turned to melancholy and I found myself awash in grief again.

Without really thinking of what I was doing, I took the yearbook as well as other articles and began collecting them in a heap. Slowly and methodically, I moved about the room repositioning furniture, removing wall hangings with cats pictured on them, and dusting and cleaning. When I was finished, I had collected two large bags full of old books and toys that she had elected to leave behind. In my mind, these artifacts filled with such powerful memories had to go. The room that once belonged to Cetra, no longer did. It now belonged to me.

For the next several months—almost a year—I went on a journey of discovery throughout the house I once shared with Cetra. I didn't know it at the time, but I was reclaiming my home as mine and mine alone. I discovered some interesting things. First, I discovered that Cetra was in every room of my house – in fact, she was in every corner, every crevice, tucked away in drawers, on my walls, in hidden places, and even on tee shirts and cut-off jeans. Funny thing is, there were some rooms she seldom entered, and yet the potency of her presence was there as much as her bedroom.

In my bedroom, in my personal nightstand, I had always kept her "A" papers and the countless certificates she'd garnered for spelling, reading, and good behavior. I had her old report cards, old geography assignments, and an assortment of quarterly performance notices from old teachers and people who had guided her life academically. Needless to say, as I read through each one, the gold stars and great big "A's" that her teachers had inscribed on each one reduced me to tears. As I discarded them, the excruciating pain associated with releasing them was mixed with an indescribable appreciation for the many people who must have experienced a grief akin to mine when they too had to release her. Their signatures were proof that they too had loved her and cherished her.

In my kitchen, I laughed out loud as I re-discovered her favorite bowl, her favorite glass and remnants of her favorite snacks. No one was allowed to eat out of these dishes but her. She was an addict when it came to Ben & Jerry's ice cream, Doritos, and Lemon-flavored Nestea. I laughed and laughed as I remembered her absolute hatred for onions. I used to sneak powdered onion into her favorite dish which was spaghetti. Once I gathered all of her compliments about how "great" the spaghetti meal was, I took great delight in telling her that I put onion powder in the meatsauce. With a sour look of disgust and a turned up nose, she'd turn on her heels and run away from me. She was a strange kid sometimes, but it also made her funny and delightful. I missed her desperately – but unbeknownst to me, my heart was going through a healing process as I released the trinkets and memories that belonged exclusively to her.

In my living room, there was a huge picture of the two of us over my fireplace, and photos of her at every stage of her life. These could stay, but the worn-out Lion King video had to go. When she was a little thing, she used to constantly stop this tape, play it, rewind it, forward it, and play it ad nauseam. She could do all of the voices and could anticipate every character's next move. Of course, this brought memories of a multitude of characters that had infatuated her as a little girl. I can remember being dragged into stores looking for the newest Mary Kate and Ashley book bag and pencils with the Little Mermaid's face twisting around the stem. This all, of course, brought laughter to my heart and huge silly grins to my face. As I handled them, and discarded them, I was able to release my Cetra, while clinging to precious memories that now moved me to peace.

In the end, and over the months, I changed every single room of my home. I discarded things, hid some things, gave some things away, and moved other things to other rooms. Now, when you walk through my house, it is my house and there is no room that I presently go into that I find painful or that reduces me to grief. Cetra is gone from my life – perhaps forever – but who she was to me and what she was to me are treasures that no earthly trinket could ever contain.

What I know forever, is that letting go is a process. You can't do it all at once and you can't do it because someone wants you to. You have to do it to take your life back and so that you can live again and laugh again. I found the whole thing to be a painful process, but I also found it extremely liberating. The irony of it all in terms of what I learned, is that the releasing was very final and few things if any tend to take me back to the former melancholy and anguish. It was an experience that was uniquely my own and is sometimes hard to share with others. Nonetheless, it absolutely restored my ability to begin living again without Cetra in my world. ♪

 *Inspiration & Hope*

Grief by any cause may ultimately lead to depression and constant crying. In letting go of an adopted child, grant yourself permission to experience each of the stages of grief for whatever it is to you – just make sure that it does not become prolonged and morose. I learned that crying and talking and even writing about Cetra helped me to face the pain of losing her in a balanced, sane way.

I don't let people try to convince me that she is coming back. I understand that this is their compassionate way of addressing my sense of loss. For me, it is a false hope that would keep me from living in a present reality.

I would much prefer that she return and that I be greatly surprised and delighted, than to want and anticipate something that may not happen for many years into a future that I cannot control. If she ever returns, neither she nor I will be the same people. Hence, in allowing myself to grieve for her as the loss of my only child, I have also given myself permission to plan and live my life anew without her in it.

Chapter 17 - A Good, Hard Cry

On the plane ride from Cetra's warden state to New York, I turned to her and asked what she wanted to call me. When she was a little bitty thing just learning to talk, my name became a hybrid between "Lane" and "Yay." At ten years old, she looked up at me with a deeply reflective face and pronounced that she wanted to call me "Mom." In all of the years that I loved her and cared for her as my little girl, she never deviated from this form of address. I could never get her to call me "Mommy" or "Mother" – it was always "Ma" or "Mom."

On the day she stopped calling me "Ma," I experienced the most chilling, heart-breaking pain I'd ever experienced. That experience was the single most important reason that I decided to write this book. I believe it is the same nameless pain that connects all adoptive parents to some degree or another.

The day it happened started out as most others did. For many, many weeks after she left my care, I had not heard a word from her. I'd tried, to no avail, to contact her at the number that her birthmother had left. I'd get an answering machine or a strange voice on the other end claiming not to have ever heard of anybody named *Cetra*. As you can imagine, my worry crystallized into dread. Where was my child? Was she safe? Was she being treated right? Why wouldn't these people answer my calls and at least tell me how my child was faring in her new environment?

On the day this dreadful silence was broken, I was resting in my home after a typically stressful day at work. The phone rang and I answered trying to distinguish the identity of a small, childish voice on the other end of the line. "May I ask who you are trying to reach?" I inquired. The small voice was unintelligible. Finally, I heard it say, "Aunt Elaine, this is Cetra."

For a second my heart lost a beat and tried to recover its rhythm. In the next second, I thought I heard glass breaking, but it was just the sound of pain screeching in my head. I managed to speak, but found that my voice was little more than a whisper. It had been nearly three months since I'd seen or heard the voice of my child. "Cetra, is this really you?" I asked. When she answered in the affirmative, I deliberately used a calm even tone of voice as I asked her to please repeat what she just called me. Knowing her as well as I do, I got a quick visual picture of the contortions her face were undergoing, as my request was met with dead silence. The mother instinct in me wanted to settle the issue and make it right for my child, but there was something in my spirit that had been bruised badly.

I repeated my request and gave her more time. At some level, I knew the demand held a latent threat, but I couldn't help myself. Haltingly, and in an audible whisper, she spoke to me, "Aunt Elaine." There was a finality to it that disturbed me, but a determination in it that disturbed me even more.

I can remember today that the conversation lasted no more than two minutes. I can remember today that the conversation was little more than Cetra voicing the demands of her birthmother for the return of a gift that Cetra had hated the moment she opened the box. I can remember Cetra's voice sounding like someone else calling from a distant land. Other than these things, the most salient memory I have of that phone call is my child addressing me as "Aunt" instead of "Ma." I believe firmly in my mind now that this is when the screaming probably first started.

There are no words to describe the disappointment and wounding, but allow me to describe the peculiar course that the pain took that day. I was so wounded. I went to sleep to try to stop the inner voices and the sound of my child calling me "Aunt." These people had taken my child many miles away in a completely new environment and had not felt that courtesy warranted a phone call about her health and welfare. They had absented themselves from her life when she needed them the most, and now they made her the chief pawn in this strange vendetta. I hurt badly and cried myself into a fitful sleep.

I remember my phone ringing again and heard the click and two second delay of the answering machine as it gives its automated message. From the distance, I thought I'd heard the familiar voice of a friend, but I had no strength to even move. Later that evening when I finally stirred, I ached all over and my head was pounding. My face felt hot and my eyes and cheeks were bloated and swollen. I felt like someone had beaten me up and took something from me. I was also hungry and made my way to the bathroom to clean up and to regain some semblance of control. There were so many emotions tumbling together in my heart and mind, that when I hit the "play" button on my answering machine for the second time, I still couldn't distinguish the caller's name or entire number.

The caller's voice nagged me because I knew it well, but hadn't heard it in a long time. I caught the area code of her number, but the rest was muffled. The message, however, was clear and filled with urgency. "Elaine," the voiced stated with stress, "I have to talk to you immediately—it is urgent. Please call me no matter how late." Then, I heard the undecipherable number and the click ending the message. I picked up the phone and dialed the operator asking her to identify the geographic source of the area code. Tennessee. The identity came to me as soon as the operator identified the state. It was Veronica—my close friend from Tennessee. I felt an overwhelming sense of helplessness immediately, even as I momentarily exalted at connecting the voice with the state of Tennessee. I felt like a deflated balloon, not only because I didn't have her number, but also because whatever she needed so urgently, I didn't have to give.

I bundled myself up against the cool evening air and drove around aimlessly looking for a quiet, dark restaurant. I didn't feel like facing people and my heart hurt so bad that I felt like a knife was protruding from it. Plus, I knew that I must look awful. When

Elaine Rose Penn

I returned home, it happened just as I pulled my car into the garage and lowered the garage door.

I had just lowered the door, when I felt a tremble move from my stomach up into my head. I was sitting in my car still, with my foot on the brake and the gear still in drive. Before I could shift to park, I felt the tremble turn into a scream. I opened my mouth to let it out, but it got stuck in my throat and wouldn't come out. I felt like I was choking on it. I started hitting my steering wheel trying to dislodge it, but it stayed there with part of its fist fastened around my heart and squeezing. I kept hitting the wheel, hoping the pressure would break it loose, but still, it wouldn't come out. The tears flowed, but the scream was a silent agony - felt but not heard.

Finally, it exploded and cut the air like a knife. It kept coming and coming and coming in waves. It continued striking the walls of the garage, until finally there was nothing left. A warning light went off in my head and from the distance I could hear a patient, kind voice talking to me. I heard it give me directions. Put your car in park, it said. Get out of your car and go into your house, it directed me. Close your door behind you and lock it, was its next command. Go to your bedroom and lie down. I followed each command and fell back into a fitful sleep, but noticed that the light on my answering machine was blinking with a signal that a new in-coming call had come in.

I jumped as I heard Veronica's voice leaving a third message of urgency. As the machine picked it up and recorded the message, I sat up on the edge of my bed weary and probably close to something akin to a nervous breakdown. Fresh tears surfaced, and I found myself cradling myself in my own arms. I sat there and did what I have done countless times in the dark moments of my life...I prayed and prayed. I prayed for peace. I prayed that the tears would stop. I prayed for calm. And...I prayed that God would please send Veronica another counselor. Tonight, I was not the one. This one only had a broken heart.

As I argued with myself about returning the call, the urgency in my friend's voice pierced my own pain. What if the trouble my friend found herself currently in was life-threatening? What if the urgency she spoke of had to do with the loss or death of someone who was dear to me? This news was either going to break me further or sharpen my resolve.

No matter what argument I tried on myself in this most perplexing state of mind, I just couldn't turn a deaf ear to a friend in need. I heard my God whisper to me to not be afraid. He said that He was with me. I knew that I had to return the call no matter what the news might cost me further on this night.

I called the number left by my friend and she answered on the first ring. I told my heart to be still and demanded that it be totally present for my friend. Whatever she was dealing with in her life was much bigger than what I was going through at that moment in my own life. This last self-rebuke seemed to work and I found that I could successfully push away my pain enough to focus on my friend.

"Elaine, how are you?" came her cheerful voice. Her tone threw me off guard. I was expecting anguish. For a second, I almost broke down to empty myself of my own sorrow, but I quickly checked myself with a reminder that my friend's problems were more important than mine. Cetra, though distant, was still alive – she was not dead – and in that fact alone, I had something good to cling to.

I became more and more disenchanted with my friend as the discussion progressed. Although I said little – I was too emotionally weary to attempt a chain of sentences – my friend kept me alert by chirping from one subject to another. Clearly, she was not in despair at all. Immediately, I regretted that I had even returned her call. I was in no mood for cheerful banter, and did not even want to talk.

She hedged several times with leading questions, trying to get me to talk. I refused to relent for fear of exploding. Finally, when I could take the suspense no more and when her banter began to fray my nerves, I spoke softly but prodding her to tell me what the urgency of her message to me had meant.

She began slowly and unsurely, almost as if she was struggling to try to keep her courage. "Elaine, you will not believe what happened a few hours ago. A friend and I were praying, when she stopped suddenly and spoke your name. Ever since she read your book on *Soulties*, she always inquires about you as if she is personally acquainted with you. When she stopped and spoke your name, there was alarm in her eyes and urgency in her voice. She said to me, 'Veronica, Elaine is in trouble. You must stop and call her right this minute. She is in trouble.' I couldn't believe what my friend was saying – as I calculated the timeline in my mind as she recounted the strange experience, I realized that at the moment at which they were praying, I must have been talking to Cetra as aunt instead of mother.

Veronica continued recounting the strange experience she had experienced with her friend. "Elaine, she saw you as if you were standing right in front of her. She described your physical features and knew things about your appearance that only someone who had met you would even notice. She told me to call you at once, but she also gave me a warning. She told me that no matter what you shared or kept to yourself that I was to listen and not try to counsel you. She said to me, *What Elaine needs is a good, hard cry.*"

With my friend close by spiritually, and prayerfully holding my hand, I wept and wept and wept until I could weep no more. The gut-wrenching intensity of my own pain surprised me. I would have thought that after all of the previous tears, nothing could be left. Something turned that day and at that moment with my friend on the other end of the line so many miles away. I thought the scream, in its raging, had ended in the garage. It had continued – silently – until this moment. Now it was spent.

My friend, Veronica, was true to the instructions given to her. And her friend was correct – it was not counsel that I wanted or needed. What I needed – at that moment – was someone with a mother's heart who wouldn't give me false assurances or trivialize the wrenching sadness of that moment. For that moment, I wanted and needed to be sad and to feel the pain. A new day would come for me when I could think of that day without the noise of pain, but for that day, I needed a good, hard cry. ♪

Inspiration & Hope

When you are a person who is accustomed to helping others, it is extremely difficult to ask for help when you are the one who is hurting. This is a terrible place of vulnerability for people who are helpers. At a most basic level, it means that you have a need to always be in control of your own emotions and to have the answers for everybody else. It also may mean that you don't allow people the privilege of just being your friend.

I have learned that while good, trusting friendships are hard to nurture and establish, they are possible if you are willing to make the investment. For some people, support groups are helpful. For me, there is nothing more liberating than the compassionate ear of a dear friend who knows when to speak and when to be silent.

Chapter 18 - A Community of Healers

Someone popularized the proverb that it takes a whole village to raise a child. That village, I've learned, is made up of some of the most diverse and unlikely people you can imagine.

What would I have done without several generations of teachers, counselors, and teaching assistants who provided guidance to my Cetra? They nurtured her, encouraged her, and cheered her on with gold stars and large A's boldly displayed at the top of her papers and exams. These nameless heroes of mine bandaged up my child's often-bruised ego and at some of the most critical moments in her development as a person. They are all there behind the veiled, precious screens of childhood survival and struggle, and I am highly indebted to each of them for assisting Cetra and I along the journey.

When Cetra was about 10 or 11, she rode a yellow bus to school each day. Over the years that she rode it, some of her bus drivers were less gracious than others, but I remember one in particular that Cetra seems to have bonded with. She would come running through the front door in a whirlwind of little-girl motion. In passing, she would tell me that her bus driver told her to tell me that, "she hoped everything would turn out well." Although I wondered what this mysterious message could mean, it never dawned on me that it could mean what it turned out to mean.

One day, while standing in the doorway to greet Cetra as she disembarked from the bus, the driver yelled out at me, "When are you due?" I looked around and behind me...was she talking to me? If she was talking about "due" as in "pregnancy due," she had to be talking to somebody else. As I stood there flabbergasted and wordless, the driver abruptly drove off leaving me standing there with my mouth open and in bewilderment. "Cetra," I demanded cautiously, "what was your bus driver talking about?" With her usual amusing candor, she looked directly into my eyes and replied in a very matter of fact tone, "I told her you were having a baby."

No wonder her driver was so concerned about my well-being! By my estimation, it had been probably 11 or 12 months that Cetra had come home telling me that her driver was making inquiries about my condition!

What a delightful surprise it was for me on the day that I met with her teachers and learning specialists to see one of my former students among them. "Professor Penn," she exclaimed, as I walked in and took a seat. I searched her face struggling to remember her, but couldn't. It had been too long and she had been one of far too many. When she spoke her name, though, it rang a bell and I recalled from a distance that she had been one of my good ones. She reminded me of my days as an adjunct professor at one of the campuses for the State University of New York, and stroked my ego by telling me that my class had been one of her best and most memorable.

We greeted with a hug, and in the few moments we had before others joined us, she shared that she was Cetra's teaching assistant and mentor. She was surprised to learn that Cetra had never even mentioned her existence to me, let alone her name. She also shared that at least twice a week when she met with all of the girls assigned to her, that Cetra would bless her in song. A song??!!! Cetra could sing? The young woman who sat before me assured me that Cetra had a wonderful voice. As it turned out, my Cetra was her little song bird.

When Cetra reached high school, her classmates and friends always amazed me. It never failed that whether we saw them in the supermarket, a WalMart, or walking down the street, they would yell out Cetra's name and wave at her. Momentarily, she would then lift her face from an ever-present book and wave back. They were girls, boys, Black and White. I was always totally amazed by this circle of young people who were acquainted with her well enough to know her name. Through visits with her teachers and guidance counselors, I learned that although many of them mocked her idiosyncrasies, in their own way, they looked out for her and cared about her in a way that those of us in the adult world could never fully understand. I fondly take my hat off to her nameless friends who acted as buddies and escorts – helping her find her way through life.

I had my community of helpers as well. I remember the many heart-talks I shared with a colleague who had adopted her baby boy from a foreign land. She and I shared some good ideas about parenting together, and on many occasions I'm sure we prayed privately for each other. I remember the woman who was a computer expert in our technology department who was raising her own teenage daughter along with the trials and tribulations that accompany the voyage. We shared many laughs, and when I last saw her, she assured me – mother to mother, that one day I would hear from my Cetra again.

Mostly, I remember the wonderful and caring community of listeners who embraced me during the months immediately following Cetra's departure. As I grieved, all of them to a person gave me permission to weep and experience the loss in my own way. Some would touch me gently on the arm, knowing that a simple touch would say more than a thousand words. Others would reassure me by recounting their own stories of parental loss and transition.

By and large, the people who helped me the most were the hundreds of New York State employees who encouraged me to compile these stories. As an inspirational speaker and motivator, I used to season my presentations with what I called *"Cetra Stories."* As I shared with them what I learned about the gifts of love and life through my journey with Cetra, I was able to connect with them at a powerful human level. I am always delighted – and it brings tears to my heart – when on occasion one of them walks up to me and asks, *"Have you heard from Cetra?"*

I am equally indebted to my own mother, my sister Crystal, each of Cetra's doctors, her caseworkers, her sitters - especially LaToya, her god-sisters, our pastors, and her surrogate aunts, uncles, moms and dads who formed a community of guardians around both of us.

Most of all, I am grateful to my God who helped us through many tears and sorrows and was there to strengthen the both of us when our journey ended and it was time to say *goodbye*. ♪

Inspiration & Hope

One of my favorite stories in Scripture involves a man whose adopted daughter became a queen. Her name was Esther. His name was Mordecai. Each year, the Jewish holy day of Purim is celebrated in Esther's honor. In the story of Esther, before she became queen, she was compelled to compete with hundreds of beautiful virgins in order to win the heart and betrothal of the king.

The story is one of my favorites because although the adoptive parent had to release his child to live her life of royalty without him, he stayed close to her in the courtyard of her life.

He watched from a distance to make sure she fared well, and from time to time he sent word to let her know that he would always be there for her in spirit and prayer as long as she needed him.

Along the way, in Esther's story, we learn of a number of people who also loved her, taught her, and guided her life's journey in the king's palace. Although Mordecai is central to her destiny as queen, he was not the only contributor or necessarily the most important. Her story should remind all of us that it takes a whole community of loving people to heal a wounded child.

The fact of the matter is, once I surrender my child to the palace, I'll need you to look after her for me and reassure her that if for whatever reason I'm not there when she cries or is in need of answers, she can count on you to show her the rest of the way.

www.ingramcontent.com/pod-product-compliance
Ingram Content Group UK Ltd.
Pitfield, Milton Keynes, MK11 3LW, UK
UKHW021322180426
11947UKWH00015B/1375